the Tennis Drill Book

TINA HOSKINS

Human Kinetics

Library of Congress Cataloging-in-Publication Data

Hoskins, Tina, 1965-
  The tennis drill book / Tina Hoskins.
    p. cm.
  ISBN 0-7360-4912-6 (soft cover)
  1. Tennis--Training. I. Title.
  GV1002.9.T7H67 2003
  796.342'2--dc21   2003009192

ISBN-10: 0-7360-4912-6
ISBN-13: 978-0-7360-4912-2

Drills 215, 217, 218, 219, 220, 221, 222, and 223 adapted, by permission, from J. Hustlar, 1993, *Munchkin Tennis PTR 1993* (Chicago, IL: Triumph Books).

Drills 236, 237, 238, 239, 240, 241, 242, and 245 from "Backboard Drills for Individuals and Groups" by Mike Bachicha and Dennis Van der Meer in *Supplement 4 PTR Instructor's Manual*. Reprinted with permission of Professional Tennis Registry, Hilton Head Island, SC.

Acquisitions Editor: Martin Barnard; **Developmental Editor:** Laura Pulliam; **Assistant Editor:** Alisha Jeddeloh; **Copyeditor:** Bob Replinger; **Proofreader:** Coree Clark; **Permission Manager:** Toni Harte; **Graphic Designer:** Robert Reuther; **Graphic Artist:** Kim McFarland; **Photo and Art Manager:** Dan Wendt; **Cover Designer:** Andrew Tietz; **Photographer (interior):** © Terry Wild Studios unless otherwise noted; **Illustrator:** Francine Hamerski; **Printer:** Versa Press

We thank Colonial Park in Somerset, New Jersey, for assistance in providing the location for the photo shoot for this book.

Human Kinetics books are available at special discounts for bulk purchase. Special editions or book excerpts can also be created to specification. For details, contact the Special Sales Manager at Human Kinetics.

Printed in the United States of America   10   9   8   7   6

Human Kinetics
Web site: www.HumanKinetics.com

United States: Human Kinetics
P.O. Box 5076
Champaign, IL 61825-5076
800-747-4457
e-mail: humank@hkusa.com

Canada: Human Kinetics
475 Devonshire Road, Unit 100
Windsor, ON N8Y 2L5
800-465-7301 (in Canada only)
e-mail: info@hkcanada.com

Europe: Human Kinetics
107 Bradford Road
Stanningley
Leeds LS28 6AT, United Kingdom
+44 (0)113 255 5665
e-mail: hk@hkeurope.com

Australia: Human Kinetics
57A Price Avenue
Lower Mitcham, South Australia 5062
08 8372 0999
e-mail: info@hkaustralia.com

New Zealand: Human Kinetics
Division of Sports Distributors NZ Ltd.
P.O. Box 300 226 Albany
North Shore City, Auckland
0064 9 448 1207
e-mail: info@humankinetics.co.nz

Thanks Dad!

1960-64 Texas Southern University
Singles Champion
Still the best player I'll ever know.

Contents

Drill Finder **vii** | *Preface* **xi** | *Acknowledgments* **xiii**
Court Diagram Key **xiv**

PART I

Strokes and Technique 1

Chapter 1   Grips 3
Chapter 2   Ground Strokes 11
Chapter 3   Volleys 25
Chapter 4   Serves and Returns 35
Chapter 5   Lobs and Overheads 53

PART II

Tactics and Strategy 59

Chapter 6   Offensive Play 61
Chapter 7   Defensive Play 69
Chapter 8   Equalizing Game Styles 77
Chapter 9   Strategic Game Planning 89
Chapter 10 Court-Surface Tactics 119
Chapter 11 Mental Mechanics 133

PART

Competition and Match Play 147

Chapter 12   Singles Games 149

Chapter 13   Doubles and Multiplayer Games. 157

Chapter 14   Match Simulation Games 165

PART

Movement and Conditioning 175

Chapter 15   Endurance Training 177

Chapter 16   In-Season Maintenance 187

PART

Competitive Group Games 201

Chapter 17   Teaching Group Games 203

Chapter 18   Backboard Drilling Games 227

Glossary   **235** | *About the Author*   **241**

Drill Finder

Grip Drills

1   Eastern Grip Technique. 5
2   Continental Grip Technique 6
3   Western Grip Technique 7
4   Semiwestern Grip Technique. 8
5   Continental-Semiwestern Grip Technique. 9

Stance Drills

6   Open-Stance Technique 13
7   Crosscourt and Down the Line. 14
8   Return of Serve 14
9   Baseline Rally. .15
10   Semiopen-Stance Technique 16
11   Neutral-Stance Technique 17
12   Closed-Stance Technique 18
13   Open-Stance Backhand Technique 19
14   Open-Stance Backhand 21
15   Ready, Set, Split Step 21
16   Crazy 8 Ground Stroke 22
17   Buggy-Whip Technique. 23

Volley Drills

18   Swinging-Volley Technique 26
19   Drop-Volley Technique 28
20   Low-Volley Technique. 29
21   Half-Volley Technique. 30
22   Approach-Volley Technique 31
23   High-Volley Technique 32
24   Split-Step Attack 33
25   No-Bounce Scoring 33
26   No-Bounce Tennis 34

Service Drills

27   Flat-Serve Technique 37
28   Slice-Serve Technique 38
29   Kick-Serve Technique 39
30   Thrust Launch Serve Technique 41
31   Squat Launch Serve Technique 42
32   Crossover Launch Serve Technique. 43
33   Flat Service 43

34   Slice Service 44
35   Kick Service 44
36   Thrust Launch Service 45
37   Squat Launch Service 45
38   Crossover Launch Service 46
39   Service Repetition. 47
40   Service Breathing 47
41   Service Balance 48
42   Service Geometric 49
43   Wide Service Interception. 49
44   Knuckle Ball. 50
45   Service Footwork 50
46   Service Motion .51
47   Service Tossing. 51

Lob and Overhead Drills

48   Topspin Forehand Lob Technique 54
49   Backhand Lob Technique 55
50   Right Ear, Left Ear 56
51   Deep Lob. 56
52   Drop and Lob 57
53   Lob and Pass 57
54   Overhead Lob Technique 58
55   Overhead Smash Technique 58

Offense Drills

56   Fast Swing. 64
57   Ball Feeding. 64
58   Minicourt. 65
59   Inside-Out Forehand 67
60   Spank That Backhand 67

Defense Drills

61   Concentrate and Play Great 70
62   Windy Day, No Problem. 72
63   Sunny Days Again. 73
64   Tiebreaker 73
65   Choke Syndrome 74
66   Changeover 75

Style Drills

67　Court Handicap 78
68　Stroke Handicap 79
69　Score Handicap 80
70　Double Cube 81
71　Tennis Football 81
72　Small Change 82
73　Net Rusher Equalization 82
74　Master Baseliner Equalization 83
75　Power Player Equalization 85
76　Baseline Counterpuncher Equalization 85
77　Pusher Equalization 86
78　Hacker Equalization 87

Strategy Drills

79　Singles Challenge 90
80　Crosscourt and Down the Line 91
81　Crazy 8 Volley 92
82　Three-Hit Cycle 93
83　Ten-Ball Singles 94
84　Up and Back 95
85　Five-Ball Overhead Sequence 95
86　Six-Ball Pattern Sequence 96
87　Criss-Cross Volley Poach 96
88　Approach, Shot, Volley, Overhead 97
89　Chip Approach and Touch Volley 98
90　Oscillation Volley .99
91　Hit the Volleyer and Run 100
92　Recovery 101
93　Quick Volley 102
94　Single-File Volley Approach 102
95　Short Ball 103
96　Crosscourt Rally Attack 104
97　Rising Star 104
98　Short Court 105
99　Deep Shot 105
100　Half-Court Hustle 106
101　Approach Shot, Passing Shot 106
102　Net Approach 107
103　Attack and Smack 107
104　Hot-Pepper Doubles 108
105　Doubles Hustle .108
106　Doubles Approach Lob and Recovery 109
107　Volley-Lob-Volley 110
108　Quick Volley Drop Out 111
109　Doubles Approach-Shot Challenge 112
110　Attack and Defend Doubles Challenge 113
111　Rotating Approach Doubles 114
112　Australian Doubles 115
113　Monster Doubles 116

114　Monkey in the Middle 117

Court-Surface Drills

115　Five-Ball Recovery 120
116　Serve and Approach Low 121
117　Traction and Balance 122
118　Hurricane 123
119　Mad Batter 124
120　Fast Grass 125
121　Make It or Break It 126
122　Return of the Big Serve 127
123　Four-Hit Serve and Volley 128
124　Hot-Pepper Singles 129
125　Advanced Singles Hustle 129
126　Three-Hit Baseline 130
127　Four-Hit Passing Shot 131
128　Two-on-One Serve and Volley 132

Mental Training Drills

129　Ball-Machine Stretch Volley 135
130　Tick-Tock 136
131　Three-on-One Passing Shot 138
132　Hardcore Ground-Stroke Volley 139
133　One Up-One Back 140
134　Two Back-One Up 141
135　Shadow Volley 141
136　Everlasting Service 142
137　Captain Hook Service 142
138　Preplanned Set .143
139　Volley Lunge 144
140　Serve and Volley 145
141　Hara-Kiri at the Net 145
142　Patterned Net Rush 146
143　Scrambled Egg 146

Singles Games

144　Tea and Biscuits Game 150
145　King or Queen of the Court Game 151
146　Rotating Singles Game 151
147　Rotating Canadian Singles Game 152
148　Tennis Blackjack Game 153
149　Mini-Me Tennis Game 153
150　Singles Attack Game 154
151　Singles Go Game 154
152　Half Courting Game 155
153　Singles Minefield Game 156

Doubles and Multi-Player Games

154　Sticky Situation Game 158
155　Out Game 158

156 Moon-Ball Game. 159
157 Survivor Game 160
158 Flub Game. 160
159 Knocker Tennis Game 161
160 Rush and Crush Game 161
161 Sink or Swim Game 162
162 Quick-Change Game 162
163 Tennis Baseball Game 163

Match Simulation Games

164 Doubles Serving Team Game 166
165 Chip-Lob Return Game 167
166 Rotating Doubles Game 168
167 Serve and Volley-Volley Game. 169
168 Medusa Passing-Shot Game 170
169 Half-Volley Passing-Shot Challenge Game . . .171
170 Overhead Smash Game 171
171 Team Merry-Go-Round Game. 172
172 Peg-Leg Doubles Game 173

Endurance Drills

173 Point and Go 178
174 Dark Shadow 178
175 Shuttle Run 179
176 Fan. 180
177 Court Circuit. 181
178 Nonstop Rally. .182
179 Run, Hit, and Recover 183
180 Step-Out Volley. 183
181 Quick-Feet Alley 184
182 Dexterity Ball 184
183 Skiing for Skill .185

Conditioning Drills

184 Deep-Chair Push-Ups 189
185 Calf Stretch 189
186 Hamstring Stretch 190
187 Posterior Shoulder Stretch 190
188 Stork Quadriceps Stretch 191
189 Leg Extension. .191
190 Leg Curl. 192
191 Leg Press. 192
192 Compound Row 193
193 Lateral Pulldown. 193
194 Overhead Press. 194
195 Chest Press 194
196 Lateral Deltoid Raise 195
197 Torso Rotation .195
198 Spinal Twist 196
199 Crunches 196

200 Speedy Interval Training. 197
201 Basic Interval Training 197
202 Cross-Training .198
203 Surface Cross-Training 199

Teaching Group Games

204 Ball Pickup Game 205
205 Me and My Shadow Game. 205
206 Oops! I Forgot My Racket Game. 206
207 Through the Target Game. 206
208 Pop-Up Volley Game 207
209 Tiger Woods Tennis Game 208
210 Tennis for Tots Game 208
211 Duck, Duck, Goose Tennis Game 209
212 Totally Tough Tennis Game 210
213 Around the Tennis World Game 210
214 Alley Rally Game. 211
215 Wacky Knees Game 211
216 Tornado Tennis Game 212
217 Highest Skyscraper Game. 212
218 Icebreaker Game 213
219 Scoop and Scoot Game 213
220 Racket Reluy Game. 214
221 Hot Potato Game 214
222 Munchkin Sez Game 215
223 Crazy Caps Game 215
224 Crazy Hitting Game 216
225 Red Light! Green Light! Game 217
226 SPUD Game. 218
227 Leap Frog Game 219
228 Crush a Bug Game 220
229 Busketball Tennis Game. 221
230 Creepy Crawly Game. 222
231 Caterpillar Game. 223
232 Lizards Have Two Skins Game. 224
233 Wonka-Wash Game 225
234 Fox and Chicken Game 226
235 Freeze-Tag Tennis Game. 226

Backboard Games

236 Key Targets Game. 228
237 Kaleidoscope Game. 228
238 Yo-Yoing Game. 229
239 Backboard Overhead Game 229
240 Poison Ivy Game. 230
241 Backboard Shadow Game 231
242 Pop-Up Game. .231
243 Rack Attack Game. 232
244 Superball Touch Game 232
245 Monkey See, Monkcy Do Game 233

Preface

Here it is!—the best collection of tennis drills, games, and tips for players and teaching pros. Drills and games are the foundation of good practice. Everyone needs them, from beginning players to veteran instructors, even ranked professionals!

As an instructor, you've probably spent countless hours discussing what students will work on each week, figuring out warm-ups, and struggling to make practice effective yet entertaining so that your students improve and enjoy themselves at the same time. With *The Tennis Drill Book* you'll never waste that time again. Instructors or players won't have to buy 10 books to find 10 different types of drills or games. *The Tennis Drill Book* contains a plethora of information that you can easily carry onto the tennis court for a quick drill or game for any skill level, class size, and age group. The book is organized so that you can quickly and easily find the drills you're looking for, with chapters covering competitive games, warm-ups, singles drills, doubles drills, strokes, strategy, challenging simulated match play, and on- and off-court conditioning drills for kids, juniors, and adults.

As a player, you have a smorgasbord of drills to help yourself, whether playing with partners, team members, tennis friends, or the old reliable backboard. You can quickly find drills for working on a particular stroke, for practicing shot combinations like serve and volley or ground-stroke patterns, or for playing against a particular game style.

All players and instructors want to play or teach to the best of their ability. The drills, games, and tips in this book will help you learn, teach, and laugh at attempts to execute shots and perform. Instructor or player, beginner or professional, young or old, tennis can hook you for a lifetime, but only if you can improve, execute, and enjoy the competition—win or lose.

ACKNOWLEDGMENTS

I am wholly indebted to the following coaches, students, colleagues, and friends for their infinite energy, professional advice, loyalty, laughter, and unstinting help in the preparation of this book: Daniel Hoskins, Bob Bynum, the staff of the Princeton Tennis Programs, all my students (you know who you are), Dr. Richard Karlen, Dick Walters, Dee Bawa, Todd Sherman, Joli Tormey, Brian Maloney, Amy Kern, Deborah Karlen-Gresh, Christopher J. Rollings, Martin Barnard, and Laura Pulliam.

Court Diagram Key

A-B-C or XXX	Players
S	Server or instructor
Ⓧ	Target
① ② or 1-2	Ball position
──────────▶	Path of players
- - - - - - - -▶	Path of ball

Strokes and Technique

The last decade of tennis has been an exciting, fast-paced race that has launched us straight into the heart of the new millennium. Players of all levels are facing hundreds of new superlength, superwide, funny-shaped featherlight rackets, bigger and lighter weight tennis balls, and serves so searingly fast that they leave skid marks where no player has left marks before. We have become lean, mean tennis machines.

But this game is no longer only for athletes with natural tennis finesse. Learning how to master the simple techniques will help players gain insight into how to perform the more advanced ones. Once players have started learning and trying to apply different techniques to their game, they will need to practice them in order to perfect them or, as we say at my club, to put their signature on them. With tennis constantly evolving, practicing helps players stay on top of their game and helps them make small changes to keep up with the competition.

The next five chapters show players how, when, and why to use the different types of grips and stances and their vital role in applying different types of spin on the ball. Practicing the many drills and tips collected in each chapter will help players master the simplest to most complicated techniques. Players will also learn how to perfect their ground strokes and volleys, how to own a penetrating overhead smash or "bomb," and how to use serving styles that fit any style of play. Remember to have fun!

chapter 1

Grips

Grips and gripping technique have changed dramatically since the 1970s and 1980s. In those years, most players used the eastern and continental grips for every stroke, giving the ball lots of power but not much spin or variety. A new era of exaggerated grips graced the 1990s, and stopping the spin, placement, and power that players use today is close to impossible.

Changing the position of the hand or hands on the grip causes the angle of the racket face to change, thereby causing the ball to spin in different directions—forward spin or topspin, backward spin or backspin, and sidespin or slice. To become more consistent and hit with controlled power, players want to put more topspin on the ball. To create a more effective volley, players want to put backspin on the ball.

With many different ways to grip the racket, from the eastern to the full western, players often overlook one aspect of gripping. Why is it that the grips do what they do? No matter what grip players choose, the part of the hand that has greater grip control will determine the depth of the shot. The palm has two ways to grip the racket—with the forefinger and thumb or with the little, ring, and middle fingers. Using the forefinger and thumb together is called using the pinchers. The bottom three fingers are called the squeezers. To achieve greater depth with the forehand and backhands, players tighten the squeezers on the forward swing. For a sharp crosscourt shot, they use the pinchers. On the forehand, the grippers are the ones controlling and tightening (which turns the grip into the eastern forehand). On the backhand, the pinchers are the control fingers and help add subtle underspin. For the serve, the grip is held loosely on the backswing. As the racket lifts to the point of contact, the pinchers tighten, rotating the forearm and snapping up to the ball for control and placement. For the volley, the continental grip is the preferred grip, but players must keep in mind that using the grippers and pinchers changes the face of the racket.

By investigating the different types of grips and knowing how to find them and use them properly, with practice players will be able to use them to build a more consistent, powerful game with reliable, sound ground strokes. Learning to use the grips of today's tennis requires excellent timing, balance, footwork, practice, and loads of patience. By using the drills collected in this chapter, players will be able to make the small changes necessary to take their game to the next level. The best grip is the most comfortable one. The player or instructor must decide which grip works best for the stroke or spin the player is trying to hit.

1—EASTERN GRIP TECHNIQUE

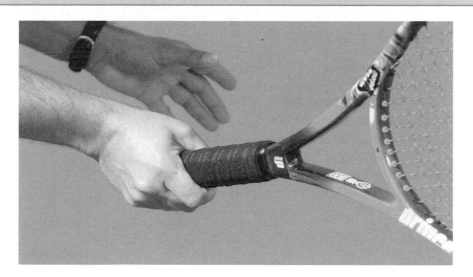

Description

The eastern grip is the standard basic grip. It is good for beginners because it is the most comfortable grip to adapt to when starting out. In addition, players can use it with forehands, backhands, serves, and volleys without having to worry about a grip change. The eastern grip is also known as the handshake grip because it is the grip most players use when picking up a racket for the first time. Players should test the grip by turning the racket so that the racket face is sideways to the net, not face down to the court. When they grip the racket handle, they should do so as though they were shaking the hand of an old friend. Before long, the eastern grip will become an old friend on the court!

Execution

Players hold the racket out in front in the left hand (or in the right hand if left handed) and rotate the racket so that the face (strings) of the racket is perpendicular to the ground. They place the palm of the free hand flat on the face of the racket and move the palm toward the body, down the shaft of the racket until it hits the end of the handle (butt). Players wrap the fingers around the grip and spread the fingers slightly apart. The thumb and forefinger should lie almost directly on the top of the grip, forming a V that points toward the right shoulder (toward the left shoulder if left-handed). The thumb should lie across the top of the grip. Players should practice the eastern grip technique with not only forehands and backhands, but also serves and volleys.

2—CONTINENTAL GRIP TECHNIQUE

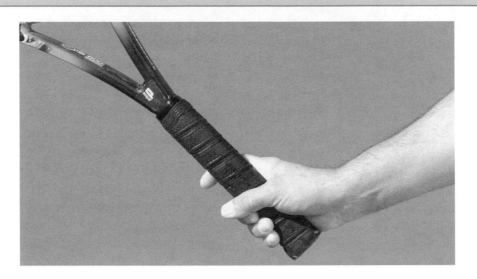

Description

Most intermediate to advanced players these days use the continental grip, sometimes called the master grip, for almost every stroke in tennis except the forehand. This one grip can create monstrous topspin, slice, and backspin on all strokes except the forehand. In using this grip to hit a forehand, the racket face is wide open to the sky, and players can make only one type of shot. In addition, the wear and tear on the wrist caused by trying to manipulate the racket isn't worth it.

Execution

Players begin by forming the eastern grip and turning the racket using the left hand if right-handed (or the right hand if left-handed). They turn the racket until it is perpendicular to the court or until it is in the twelve o'clock position. Now, right-handers turn the racket to the eleven o'clock position; left-handers turn the racket to one o'clock. Players wrap the fingers around the shaft of the racket and spread them slightly apart. The V formed by the thumb and forefinger should point toward the player, and the thumb should lie along the length of the handle. The bottom knuckle of the index finger should lie right on the top of the racket.

Tip

Players who are losing the ability to place the ball may be tightening the grip at the wrong time. They should check to see if they are tightening the grip just before striking the ball. The grip should tighten as the forward swing begins.

3—WESTERN GRIP TECHNIQUE

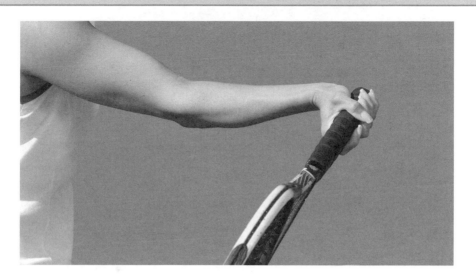

Description

The western grip is excellent for the forehand and the swinging volley. Players will generate tremendous power and spin while using this grip. Because the racket face is closed, or turned down to the court, players must explosively brush up the back of the ball while hitting the ball from low to high to get it up and over the net. This kind of swing creates topspin, and the faster players swing or brush up, the more power and spin they create.

Execution

Players start by holding the racket with an eastern grip. They relax the grip and turn the racket counterclockwise until the top of the racket is in the two o'clock position (left-handed players should turn the racket to the eleven o'clock position). They wrap the fingers around the grip and space them slightly apart. The V formation should point to the right (or to the left for left-handers), and the thumb should lie across the top of the handle. The grip should be loose until the backswing begins and then tighten when the racket strikes the ball. Keeping the grip loose prevents tension from interfering with a smooth motion.

Tip

Players should learn the fundamentals of all gripping techniques. Each player will eventually develop a style and grip as unique as his or her signature.

4—SEMIWESTERN GRIP TECHNIQUE

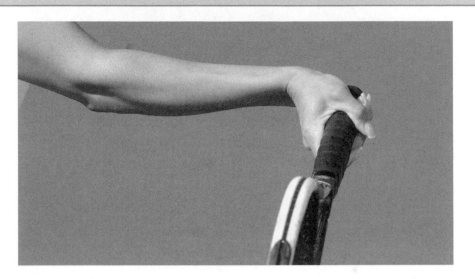

Description

This grip will achieve maximum topspin and control over shots. Players at every level can use this grip because it is so close to the handshake grip. With just a slight grip change, most players can adapt to it with minimal frustration and add topspin to the ball. The semiwestern grip is also the preferred grip against hard-court baseliners because it permits quick grip changes between the forehand and backhand grips.

Execution

Players hold the racket using the western grip and point it in the two o'clock position if right-handed, in the eleven o'clock position if left-handed. To achieve the semiwestern grip, players turn the grip back to one o'clock if right-handed, or between eleven o'clock and twelve o'clock if left-handed. When using this grip right-handers must follow through into the left hand. Left-handers must follow through into the right hand. The tracking hand or free hand or nonracket hand is the hand that changes the grip. For example, right-handed players positioned to hit a forehand ground stroke when the ball is on their side of the net point to the incoming ball with the left hand, stroke the ball out to a targeted area of the court, and then complete the follow-through by swinging the racket (grip) into the left hand. Both hands should be on the racket (grip) and ready for the next shot.

5—CONTINENTAL-SEMIWESTERN GRIP TECHNIQUE

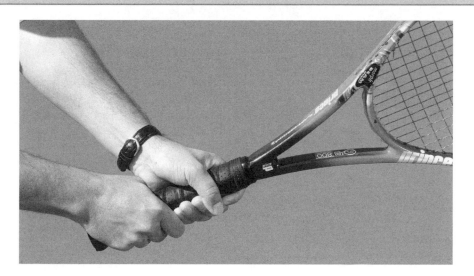

Description
By using a combination of the continental and semiwestern grips, players can generate heavy topspin, have maximum control, and develop wicked power with their ground strokes. Players who prefer to hit with a two-handed backhand or forehand prefer this grip combination.

Execution
Right-handers place the right hand in the continental grip and then place the left hand above the right hand on the grip. Making sure that both hands are touching lightly, they place the left hand in the semiwestern grip position. Left-handers use the reverse process. Players must remember never to release a hand off the grip until they complete a full follow-through.

Variation
The eastern grip, eastern–semi-western grip, and continental-eastern grip may be used for both the two-handed backhand and forehand ground stroke.

Tips
Players may sometimes have to use different grips for the different types of balls hit at them on a particular surface, even by the same opponent. Players must be able to adapt to all situations. No single grip is acceptable at all times for each stroke.

A great way for players to develop the racket head speed needed to generate wicked power with ground strokes is to release the bottom hand (this hand controls the stroke) and simply hit forehands while keeping their grip in its original position.

chapter 2

Ground Strokes

The definition of sound ground stroking begins with how players approach an incoming tennis ball. Players can use either a forehand or a backhand to hit ground strokes—shots hit from baseline to baseline. Nowadays players are using two hands not only for the backhand grip but also for their forehands. Every part of the body is involved in returning a tennis ball successfully. For example, if players attempt to hit a shot crosscourt but the ball flies up and over the back fence, their first thought may be that they are hitting the ball too hard or just don't have the finesse it takes to control the ball. The problem isn't too much strength or lack of finesse, it's the approach to the ball and what happens when players actually strike the ball. If players lift the chin or head while striking the ball, the ball will follow the head and fly high. If players straighten the front leg, meaning that they don't keep both knees down while hitting, chances are the ball will sail over the fence. Many factors affect the direction and control of the ball, which ultimately effects players' ability to hit effective ground strokes. The first stop on the road to successful ground stroking is moving the feet and stepping into the ball while using the most effective stance.

A stance is both an individual and a natural extension of a style of play. The stance for any shot is influenced by the player's position on the court, the difficulty of the oncoming ball, the grip, and the player's physical conditioning. Thus, four different hitting stances used in today's wickedly fast-paced tennis determine the player's level or potential level. During the 1970s and 1980s it was virtually unheard of to use the open stance in anything but an emergency, but the fast pace of the game today has dramatically reversed previous beliefs. One cannot play today's tennis using the stepping-across or closed-stance footwork to execute a counter against balls coming in at speeds greater than 100 miles per hour. The speed and power of professional tennis has dictated the need for players to "conform" their games in an attempt to combat the intensity at which the game is now played.

Thus, the open and semiopen stances are a product of today's power game. The widespread use of the semiwestern and full western grips has allowed players to generate tremendous racket power and speed from the semiopen and open stances. Players should adapt the use of both based on their personal style of play, use of various grips, movement skills, and stage of development.

During match play, players will have to use a preferred stance and sound ground stroking in all sorts of difficult situations, depending on the speed, spin, and direction of the opponent's shot. In any case, players should remember the basic rules for proper footwork and combine them with good, solid ground strokes. This chapter will help players become familiar with the four different hitting stances. Sound ground-stroking rules combined with drills will help players perfect their overall ground-stroking game.

6-OPEN-STANCE TECHNIQUE

Description

The open stance is perfect for situations when little time is available to prepare because the combination of stepping out, shifting body weight to the outside foot, loading the hip, and turning the trunk lessens preparation time. Players can hit killer forehands and backhands from this stance because they can load up on the outside hip and virtually explode into the selected shot.

Execution

From the ready position, which is the starting point on the court usually behind the center (T) on the baseline, players begin the backswing by rotating the shoulders and hips simultaneously, stepping out to the right with the right foot if right-handed, and shifting the weight to the outside foot, the right foot. With weight on the outside foot, players should remain balanced through the follow-through and recovery. Because the shoulders, trunk, and hips are coiled like a tightly wound spring, after beginning the stroke players will uncoil with tremendous speed. This uncoiling action helps players hit the ball way out in front of the body, which creates great control and power.

Tip

Players should avoid shifting their body weight too early, which results in pulling off the ball too early and causes shots to fall short in the court or in the net. Players should remember to keep their non-hitting hand, which is commonly referred to as the ball-tracking hand, extended out to the targeted area of the court. This small but major adjustment is the key to acquiring height and depth on all shots.

7–CROSSCOURT AND DOWN THE LINE

Objective
This drill helps players groove their ground strokes, hit in a specific direction to a targeted area on the court, and focus on keeping the ball in play, thereby increasing consistency.

Execution
Players take a position at the service-line center (T). A server feeds balls. Players hit crosscourt past the service line, remembering to rotate the shoulders, trunk, and hips together to get a smooth stroke. They try to make as many shots as possible out of 10 and then repeat the drill hitting down the singles sideline.

Tip
A serious tennis player must have a potent forehand. At the same time, not every forehand must be hit at 200 miles per hour. The forehand should also be used as a controlling tool to manage the tempo and pattern of a point. A player can hit 5 or 10 or more shots to set up the point and then unleash the forehand weapon!

8–RETURN OF SERVE

Objective
This drill helps players learn how to control the spin, depth, pace, and placement of their returns with more confidence.

Description
Practicing return of serve while using the open hitting stance will raise a player's game to new levels. This simple yet effective drill isolates this specific stroke and footwork and helps players focus only on moving to the ball using this hitting stance.

Execution
Players practice hitting the return of serve using the open stance. The server hits medium-paced serves to the forehand and backhand. Players hit crosscourt past the service line and repeat the drill hitting down the line. Practicing hitting returns using the open-stance forehand or backhand will result in control of a higher percentage of points during the opponent's service game.

Tip
To serve or return effectively, players should mix up placement and spins. By serving to the corners as well as down the center (T), they can keep the opponent guessing. Many weak off-center hits are a result of rising up at the waist. Players must be sure to use their legs with a knee bend and hip rotation.

9–BASELINE RALLY

Objective
This simple, effective drill helps players learn how to use the uncoiling of their upper bodies and the proper footwork while they practice hitting when using the open hitting stance.

Description
This type of drill takes the pressure off players as they learn to control the depth and speed of their shots while using the open hitting stance. Players practice hitting past the service line, keeping weight transfer into the ball consistently forward and learning to keep shots deep in the backcourt rather than in the midcourt area where the opponent can move in and take control.

Execution
By rallying with a partner from the baseline while hitting the forehand in an open stance, players learn how to execute the open-stance footwork. Players should try rallying crosscourt, hitting forehands in an open stance and remembering to hit the ball past the service line to prevent the opponent from moving in and smacking a winner. They should repeat this drill down the line. After mastering the stance, players can play out a few points. The first player to 21 wins.

Variation
Players should also practice returning serves using the open-stance technique for both the forehand and backhand return of serve and the swinging-volley technique, while learning to control the ball in the mid-court area. Using the service boxes only, players should try to keep a continuous rally of 10 or more balls in play while using the open-stance technique on both the forehand and backhand ground strokes.

Tip
Simultaneous rotation of the shoulders and hips creates tremendous power. When they set up to hit a forehand or backhand ground stroke, players should imagine that the upper torso is a tightly coiled spring. When they release the spring without hesitation, a smooth, powerful stroke results. If players interrupt the uncoiling by breaking up the fluidity of motion, the stroke will be choppy and cause an uncontrolled return.

10–SEMIOPEN-STANCE TECHNIQUE

Description

The semiopen stance is based on the same principles as the open stance. Players use this stance when they have little time to prepare for an incoming shot. Instead of stepping forward toward the net, players open up the step slightly more to the left if right-handed, load all their weight onto the outside hip (right hip), and uncoil explosively into the forehand or backhand ground stroke.

Execution

From the ready position players begin the backswing for the forehand by rotating or coiling the hips, trunk, and shoulders simultaneously. They step out and shift their weight to the outside foot, which is the right foot for a right-hander. As with the open stance, the key to the semiopen stance is how far players step into the court with the left foot. For the semiopen stance players step slightly to the left of the net tape with the left foot to maintain a solid foundation after striking the ball. Players should remember to keep body weight on the outside foot until after contact and remain balanced during follow-through and recovery. The slight difference between the semiopen and open stance is the length of the step forward into the ball with the left foot for right-handers (with the right foot for left-handers) when hitting either a forehand or backhand.

Tip

For more control, players should hit the ball back in the direction it came from. Players must have confidence in their strokes to step outside the rally and change the direction, spin, and speed of a ball coming into the playing area at 70 or 80 miles per hour.

11–NEUTRAL-STANCE TECHNIQUE

Description

The forehand and backhand neutral stance serves as the origin for all other stances. The neutral stance allows players in the early stages of development to experience shifting weight and body rotation toward the target area. The neutral stance provides the best foundation from which to execute follow-through and recovery from shots unless a difficult ball must be played on the run. In that situation players will most likely use the semiopen or full open stance. The neutral stance is also the preferred stance to hit both one-handed and two-handed backhands because it allows players to move their weight in the direction of the targeted area.

Execution

From the ready position, players begin the backswing by rotating or coiling the hips, trunk, and shoulders simultaneously. Footwork begins by stepping out with the right foot if right-handed and shifting weight to the outside foot. Players step forward toward the center net tape with the inside foot, the left foot, and shift weight onto it before executing the forward swing. When striking the ball toward the target area of the court, they keep their weight on the front foot until after contact and remain balanced during the follow-through and recovery. Bringing the back foot forward and around, complete with a ready hop, will help maintain a strong, balanced foundation as players recover by rotating the shoulders and hips.

Tip

Teaching or using the neutral-stance technique when hitting forehands and backhands allows players of all levels to learn how to benefit from shifting their body weight smoothly forward in the direction of the targeted area of the court.

12–CLOSED-STANCE TECHNIQUE

Objective

This drill identifies the pros and cons in using this specific hitting stance for the backhand or forehand ground stroke.

Description

The closed stance is the settled-upon stance when chasing down a ball on a full run for either the backhand or forehand. Players use this stance only when forced wide for a shot or when on the run and unable to set up for quick recovery.

Execution

Players should not use this stance unless absolutely necessary. The stance closes out the hips, preventing hip rotation into the stroke and precluding transfer of weight toward the targeted hitting area. This action forces players to take additional recovery steps before they can rotate their shoulders and hips into the shot. The stance also limits control of shots, reduces shot options and power, and slows recovery time significantly.

Tip

To avoid being caught off balance, which may lead to using the closed stance, players must remember to breathe. Breathing relaxes the entire body, permitting better and quicker footwork, more racket-head speed through contact, and more pace and depth on shots. Breathing during and between points is the best way to combat the nerves or butterflies all players feel under pressure. Players should exhale as they begin moving the racket forward to strike the ball all the way through the shot. Breathing through the shot helps players avoid the tendency to hold their breath, which can lead to an overall tightness of the muscles, slower reflexes, and lazy footwork.

13—OPEN-STANCE BACKHAND TECHNIQUE

Description

The backhand is the most natural motion of any of the strokes in tennis and is ideal for both single- and double-handed players. Adding the open-stance technique to the footwork allows the backhand to become a weapon!

Execution

Whatever their size and strength, players must develop a smooth, fluid swing free from hesitation during any part of the stroke. The backswing should be one continuous motion, not a double pump or in some instances a double pump of the wrist. Simultaneous coiling of the hips, trunk, and shoulders produces fluidity, control, and power. Players must remember to load up their weight on the left foot, if right-handed, and coil the hips, trunk, and shoulders. Players often transfer their weight from the left foot to the right foot too early during the stroke. This action results in pulling off the shot too early, causing mis-hits. To have a strong foundation, players must remember to turn the shoulder before the ball crosses the net and keep their weight on the left foot throughout the stroke. After contact they extend the arm and racket out to the target for better control and depth.

Tip

The two-handed backhand is a deadly weapon for balls that sit up (sitters). Players who prefer to play using the two-handed backhand grip should look out for sitters and then move in and crunch them! Players must refrain from peeking at their shots before they complete the stroke. Trying to sneak a look will result in loss of power and depth and may cause a mis-hit. No matter which stance or grip combination they choose to use, players must learn how to anticipate the direction, speed, and height of the oncoming ball. Players must be able to get to the ball faster, return the shot with a potent shot, and recover quickly to prepare for the next shot.

Martina Hingis
Bone-Chilling Backhand

Martina Hingis, born on September 30, 1980, is five feet, seven inches tall and weighs 130 pounds. She plays right-handed with a two-handed backhand. Before deciding to call it quits in 2002, Hingis won 31 titles. Known by many as an ice queen, she had a backhand that sent chills down the spine of most players on the WTA tour. Under the watchful eye and tutelage of her coach, her mother Melanie, Martina had arresting movement and definite preparedness when she decided it was her day to play. Although some of her competitors may have hit the ball harder, no one on the tour had more flawless shots on any court or court surface. Hingis's precise blend of angles, depth, and consistency made her the leading woman player of the late 1990s. Martina attained the WTA world ranking of number 87 in 1994, number 16 in 1995, number 4 in 1996, and number 1 in 1997. When this talented young player decided to retire in 2002, she was ranked number 2 in the world. Martina amassed 25 singles titles, 25 doubles titles, 5 singles Grand Slam titles, and 7 doubles Grand Slam titles, with 2 ITF singles tiles sprinkled on top for good measure. If one were to ask Martina, who incidentally was named after Martina Navratilova, what her most memorable accomplishments were in tennis, she would say, "Winning my first WTA tour title in Filderstadt 1996, winning my first singles Grand Slam at the Australian Open in 1997, and then defending my Grand Slam title at the Australian Open in 1998." Oh yeah, and she might mention one day winning a major horseback riding and jumping competition with one of her three horses, Velvet, Sorrenta, or Montana.

14–OPEN-STANCE BACKHAND

Objective
This drill improves timing and imparts power and topspin from the fast uncoiling action of the lower body.

Description
When using the open stance and executing the backhand ground stroke, players must prepare quickly to set up for the incoming ball. This drill helps players accomplish a quick setup and an explosive follow-through.

Execution
Players take a position just inside the baseline and use the open stance while a partner serves from behind the service line. Players bend their knees and load up with their weight on the hitting-side leg. In working on quick hitting and recovery, players should remember that they have little time to step into the ball. The open stance allows players to contact the ball sooner and farther in front of the body, leaving no time for an opponent to set up and hit a blistering return.

Tip
Good running shots are as much about timing and athletic ability as they are about textbook ground-stroke construction. When on the run, players should play it safe. A backhand topspin lob or passing shot may offer the best chance to stay in the point.

15–READY, SET, SPLIT STEP

Objective
This drill helps players make the split step second nature.

Description
The split step is a dynamic move that takes players from the ready position to an explosive movement toward the ball. Every time the opponent strikes the ball, players should split step, reacting as a sprinter does after the sound of the starter's pistol. The wider the split step, the better the player's balance.

Execution
Players position the left arm in front for balance and take the racket back early. The left shoulder and arm must begin to rotate and clear the way so that the right arm can swing through the ball. Because players are running, they can't transfer weight forward into the shot. Instead, weight and momentum are moving to the side. The left foot will have moved to the side, so the hips can't open, limiting shoulder rotation. To ensure good hip and shoulder rotation on the forehand side, right-handed players should try to take their last step with the right foot before making contact.

16–CRAZY 8 GROUND STROKE

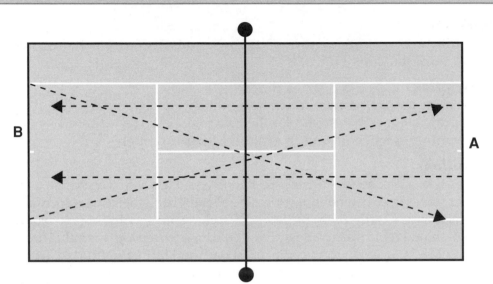

Objective

This simple ground-stroking drill builds players' confidence, consistency, direction, and ball control while using the open hitting stances. No scoring is needed because this drill is for learning, not competing.

Description

Two to four players can do this drill. Players get a sense of how to move side to side while using the different hitting stances and directing the ball to a designated area of the court without the pressure of trying to win the point.

Execution

Players A and B start at the center baseline (T) at opposite ends of the court and start rallying. Player A hits every ball down the line, and player B hits every return crosscourt. The players try to keep 20 balls going without missing. They should not compete because this is a learning drill that should be performed free of stress.

Variation

Player A takes a position at the baseline. Player B is up at the net. Player A hits every ball down the line, and player B hits every volley crosscourt. They try to keep a steady pace on the ball. To improve consistency and ball control, they hit as many balls as they can. After 10 minutes they switch directions. Players do not use scoring for this drill.

Tip

Players should try to kiss their shoulders. This technique has been phrased in many different ways, but the outcome is the same. Players often fail to complete the stroke after hitting the ball. They feel that once their rackets connect with the ball, that's all there is. But they must continue stroking out until they can place the racket (grip) into the nonhitting hand.

17–BUGGY-WHIP TECHNIQUE

Description

Pete and Steffi Graf are now hitting what's considered a reverse forehand, also known as the buggy whip. This stroke can be particularly effective when players have been stretched out wide and have no time to step into or shift body weight forward. In this situation players must hit a shot from behind the hip and follow through along the same side of the body. Right-handers normally follow through out in front and to the left side of the body and into the left hand. With the buggy whip, the follow-through whips up past the right ear, which is on the same side as the forehand stroke. It's called the buggy whip because players have to boogie to get to the ball and then whip it to get it up over the net.

Execution

The point of contact is late and low, so instead of driving completely through the shot, the racket comes up and over the same shoulder. The ball must be hit from an open stance or it won't work. Most of the body weight is on the back foot, and little weight transfer occurs because the stroke is wristy—just a whip of the racket. Players are on a full run, with no time to stop and set up, so they must whip quickly to lift the ball over the net.

Tip

Players must keep their eyes on the ball, focusing on its spin. If they don't focus long enough, they will mis-hit. To get a really good look at the ball, players must keep their heads down long enough on ground strokes and up long enough on serves and overheads.

chapter 3

Volleys

When two or more players are rallying back and forth across the net and a player achieves the goal of gaining control of the net by hitting an approach shot off the opponent's short shot, the next shot up at the net will be the volley. The technique of the volley is much less complex than that of the forehand, backhand, and serve because the movement is less complicated, but being exact is extremely important.

Volleying used to be as easy as putting one foot in front of the other. The technique just wasn't as elaborate as that required to hit ground strokes. The stroking technique of the basic volley is the same on either side of the body, except that on the backhand, as on ground strokes, contact must occur farther out in front of the body than it does on the forehand.

Players can hit volleys with either one or two hands on the racket grip. But with the excessive spin and speed of most shots, it takes a lot more than a split step, cross step, and a short, abrupt punch. The adjustments needed to hit an aggressive volley must be quick and precise. An essential part of aggressive volleying is using the continental grip and, in some instances, the full western grip. Both of these advanced volleying grips help players achieve mind-blowing speed and spin. This chapter explains the styles, technique, and drills that will help players successfully integrate volleying into their game.

18 — SWINGING-VOLLEY TECHNIQUE

Description

Not for the cowardly, this aggressive and offensive forehand and backhand weapon occurs out of a rally when players step into the area known as no-man's-land to pick off a deep ground stroke in the air. The difference between this shot and the classic volley is that the racket head is not cocked high above the wrist and the shot is hit with tremendous topspin. It's easier to think of this shot as a ground stroke from the midcourt taken out of the air before the ball bounces, and hit only with mind-numbing speed, topspin, and confidence.

Execution

The grip should be semiwestern to full western. When moving into the midcourt area to attempt this stroke, players should not hesitate in coming forward. Right-handers attempting to hit a forehand swinging volley should coil the shoulders, trunk, and hips while moving forward. They position the left hand out in front to track the ball and keep weight and momentum moving forward. The right elbow should be close to the body to shorten the backswing. The racket face is slightly closed, with the top of the racket head lower than the wrist. Once within hitting range, players should go ahead and let loose into the ball, remembering to keep the wrist loose to put lots of topspin on the shot. Players should accelerate on contact way out in front of the body with a complete follow-through. If they push the ball from inside the baseline area, the opponent will have a field day. Because of the aggressive nature of the technique, confidence is key. Encourage players not to hold back once they've mastered the basics. After hitting the swinging volley, players close to the net for a possible return.

Tip

Players should remember to use the semiwestern or full western grip when hitting using this stroke. They should be sure to practice this technique with both forehands and backhands. Perhaps most importantly, acceleration is a must! No bones about it, if you pat the ball or push the ball you may be "eating" the ball later. After the swinging volley is hit, close in on the net for possible return shot.

Andre Agassi

Explosive Swinging Forehand Volley

Born on April 29, 1970, Andre turned pro in 1986 at age 16 and was ranked third in the world by age 18. Agassi plays right-handed and has a deadly two-handed backhand. I believe that Andre made this highly advanced shot an official stroke and increased its popularity. Watching how he attacks any ball is a remarkable sight, but the way he builds up his points to step inside the midcourt area and smack a volley out of nowhere is something special. He doesn't hit just any kind of volley; he smacks a smoking forehand swinging volley loaded with topspin crosscourt for a fall-down crying winner.

Although he picked up many derogatory nicknames during his career, Agassi proved his doubters wrong when he won the U.S. Open in 1994. After undergoing wrist surgery, laying off junk food, and hiring Brad Gilbert as his new coach, Agassi blew through the 1994 tournament, playing the best tennis of his life. He beat five players ranked higher than he was, something no one had done in about 40 years. After Andre clobbered Michael Stich in the singles final, he went on to beat Pete Sampras in the 1995 Australian Open. I guess all those hitting sessions with Bjorn Borg, Ilie "Nasty Boy" Nastase, and Bobby Riggs paid off.

19—DROP-VOLLEY TECHNIQUE

Description

For forehand, backhand, and two-handed volleyers, the drop volley can be a valuable shot. This volley is especially useful when the opponent takes a position deep behind the baseline or uses an extreme western grip and has trouble switching or moving forward. A drop volley works very well because it forces the opponent to respect the player's use of finesse and touch shots in the short court area.

Execution

For this volley, players must incorporate the catch concept. Just as a baseball glove absorbs the pace of the ball on a catch, the face of the racket can absorb the pace of the ball. Players must be prepared at the contact point for the volley and eliminate any forward movement that would create a follow-through. When contacting the ball, players should allow the grip and wrist to flex with just enough power to send the ball a few feet over the net. Players should practice using the forehand and backhand drop-volley technique by hitting sharp angles to a specified area on the court. Attempting to use this technique before gaining confidence when executing the drop volley may lead to a mis-hit and will allow the opponent to move in and take advantage of the attempted shot and point. This shot requires a lot of practice to build up the confidence and touch needed for successful execution.

Tip

The drop volley is one of those finesse shots that take many hours of hitting to perfect. The key to hitting an effective drop volley is to loosen the grip just before impact and make sure that the opponent is way off balance. Otherwise, he or she will read the shot and blast a passing shot for a winner.

20—LOW-VOLLEY TECHNIQUE

Description

This volleying technique and practice drill is for forehand, backhand, and two-handed backhand volleyers attempting to retrieve and hit an effective low volley. This technique takes patience, balance, and good hand-eye coordination. Just getting down low enough and holding the body steady while moving forward is hard enough. Players must combine all that with an effective return so that the opponent won't eat up the return volley.

Execution

If time is available, players should step forward into this volley using a neutral stance. A strong foundation with a deep knee bend is key to getting down to the level of the ball. Keeping the upper body straight will improve balance and allow players to use little or no backswing on the low volley. Before contact, the racket face is slightly open, using the continental grip, to help lift the ball over the net with underspin. The underspin or backspin will help the ball die when it hits the ground. The opponent will have trouble trying to get under the ball if the shot has a lot of backspin. The shot should have little or no follow-through. If players swing, they will hit the ball too deep and the opponent will be able to get to it and hit a passing shot. The racket should remain above the wrist throughout the shot for optimum control. Dropping the racket head will put the ball in the bottom of the net.

Tip

Players should try to hit high, deep lob volleys right over the opponent's backhand side. If the opponent returns it, players should be up at the net waiting to cream the attempted return.

21 — HALF-VOLLEY TECHNIQUE

Description

The half volley, especially the forehand half volley, is one of the most difficult shots in tennis. The half volley is a stroke that players are forced to hit when the ball is aimed at their feet. It mimics a hard-hit ground ball in baseball that bounces at the feet of the shortstop. The half volley is somewhere between a volley and a ground stroke. Essentially, this means that players take neither a full ground-stroke swing nor an abrupt punch-volley stroke. Players normally don't choose to hit this shot. It chooses them, so they must be prepared!

Execution

Usually this shot happens when players are moving forward to hit an approach volley, but it can happen anywhere on the court. Players must move to the ball and not wait for it to come to them. They must keep their eyes locked in on the ball and not look away as it lands immediately in front of the feet. The shot demands perfect timing and must be hit in front of the body. Players should be positioned as low as the ball is and hold the position until the ball leaves the racket. Attempting to stand up or lift up while executing this shot will cause the ball to go into the net. By staying down and steady, players will never be surprised by the half volley.

Tip

Because the half volley is a defensive shot, the best play is to block the ball back deep and then move closer to the net. Players should hit the shot out in front, stutter or split step, and keep moving to the ball.

22—APPROACH-VOLLEY TECHNIQUE

Description

The approach volley can be hit on either side of the body, forehand or back-hand. The approach volley is sometimes known as the transitional volley because in attacking the net, players may be faced with a first volley that they are not in position for or are not ready to end the point with. Players usually encounter this volley at the service line while attempting to charge the net either after a return of serve or after they serve and attempt to rush the net.

Execution

The approach volley requires an instant grip change to the continental grip. When approaching the net, players should split step to stop the body from moving and hitting while running. They should step into the shot, keep the hips and knees down, keep the head steady throughout the stroke, and volley the shot well out in front of the body. Players should use the opponent's power, maintain strong footing, and direct the ball down the line or, if in the center of the court, down the middle. They close in and look to finish the point with the volley. An approach volley requires perfect balance and timing. Players can practice a series of serve and approach volleys or a return of serve and a move up to hit the next shot as an approach volley. They should try 25 serve and approach volleys and 25 return of serve and approach volleys.

Tip

This drill gives players extra practice on the split step or check pause before they hit the approach volley and helps develop the feeling of closing in toward the net on the finishing volley.

23 — HIGH-VOLLEY TECHNIQUE

Description

Is it an overhead or high volley? It's somewhere in between. Taken on either side, forehand or backhand, a common mistake on a high forehand or backhand volley is to swing at it. When players are positioned at the net they must punch through this volley. They must be careful in swinging at this sneaky shot, or they will knock the ball right out of the tennis stadium.

Execution

The player takes a position up at the net, and a practice partner takes a position behind the opposite service line or baseline. In learning how to identify the high volley, players should alternate playing low volleys, shoulder-high volleys, and then high volleys, which they can reach without having to back up or jump vigorously. They should try to hit 50 low volleys, 50 shoulder-high volleys, and 50 high volleys, alternating between the forehand and backhand volley. They should then try a set of 150 alternating volleys, concentrating on moving forward so that they can successfully hit through the shot. They should keep the grip tight, the wrist cocked high, and the left hand out in front for balance (if right-handed). Players then punch or block the incoming ball.

Tip

Players should keep the racket cocked high above the wrist and lock the wrist to keep it firmly in place. Players should keep their non-hitting hand extended out in front and finish into that hand after they hit the volley, mimicking a clapping motion. This action aids in balance and tracking of the ball and will keep the high-volley stroke short, sweet, and crisp.

24—SPLIT-STEP ATTACK

Objective
This drill helps players acquire good volleying form, learn to anticipate the opponent's next shot, and react aggressively.

Description
To perform the split step, players bring their feet together momentarily as they determine the direction of the opponent's shot.

Execution
Players observe the position of the opponent's shoulders and speed and direction of movement. Players then split step so that the feet touch the court when the opponent strikes the ball. The key is figuring out whether the opponent is going to pass down the line, hit crosscourt, or lob. If players hit to the opponent's forehand, he or she will be running parallel to the net with the shoulders sideways and set up to hit a down-the-line passing shot. If moving fast, the player may hit a lob because he or she will be unable to generate power. On a short approach shot or first volley, the opponent will be moving forward with the leading shoulder pointed crosscourt. A crosscourt shot is likely. When the opponent moves back to cover a deep shot, players should back up to cover because the opponent's shot will be weak enough for players to close in and smack a winning volley.

25—NO-BOUNCE SCORING

Objective
No-bounce scoring encourages aggressive play that will solidify volleying techniques used in doubles or singles. The drill creates monstrous confidence and anticipation of shots, and if players like this drill as much as my students do, it will create little monsters!

Description
When playing singles or doubles, players can score a point only by hitting a volley of any kind or an overhead. The ball may bounce to set up the points, but players score a point only if they take the ball out of the air.

Execution
Players play a regular game of singles and serve in the court they are serving in until the first point is successfully won. The player must continue serving until he or she wins the service game. The first game may take up to 10 minutes. Players can play an entire set this way.

Variation
Players can play a 12-point tiebreaker or doubles using this method.

26 – NO-BOUNCE TENNIS

Objective

This drill improves reflex action at the net, footwork, dexterity, and confidence in attacking the net. Players learn to create and recognize opportunities to attack and be successful at the net.

Description

This twist will sharpen players' attacking skills and force them to approach the net because they can't score a point unless they hit a volley successfully.

Execution

Player A is positioned on the service-line center, and player B is positioned on the opposite service-line center. Player A starts the point by drop hitting the ball to player B. Each player serves four points or an entire regular-scoring game. The ball can bounce only on the serve. Players win points only by hitting a volley, swinging volley, or overhead. Servers switch after every game or every fourth point and play 16 no-bounce points.

Variation

Players position themselves on the baseline, serving in the regular overhand way to start the point. They can play doubles using this technique.

Tip

Serving and volleying is an aggressive tactic that helps players get quickly up to the net to end and win the point. Quick hands and quick feet produce crisp, sweet volleys.

chapter 4

Serves and Returns

One hundred and fifty miles per hour! Wow, sound great? In a big match no shot is more important than the serve, the stroke that puts the ball in play. The serve can be an important offensive weapon. For example, a well-placed wide serve to the forehand or backhand will draw the opponent off the court and open it up for an easy volley winner.

Unfortunately, many players spend little time developing this important stroke. The most successful servers on the professional tour have put in thousands of hours practicing everything from tossing, standing, bending, and exploding up and into their serves to experimenting with grips. Because of this they all use a similar technique that helps them generate unbelievable spins and speed. By arranging their bodies under the toss and angling themselves as if they were throwing an upward pitch with an explosive drive up to the ball, they lean into the court using their entire body weight and snap their wrist to produce thunderous power. No matter the level of player or style, the serve can be the crucial key to determining the outcome of a closely contested match. Players should perfect each and every tiny step from ball toss, knee bend, launch, and wrist snap to the often-overlooked placement of the serve. The serve is the one and only shot in tennis that all players have complete and absolute control over, so use it skillfully!

The first and most important adjustment that players must make to learn correct service technique is the grip, which provides support to players' wrist when they are learning the basic service motion. Applying spin to the serve will help players control the ball and put a higher percentage of serves into play. Good servers also know that the contact point commands the successful serve and that by varying the contact point they can achieve different types of serves and spins. Players can use the clock method as a tool to compare where the toss should be visually (see the following clock diagram). This example is for right-handers; left-handers use the reverse pattern.

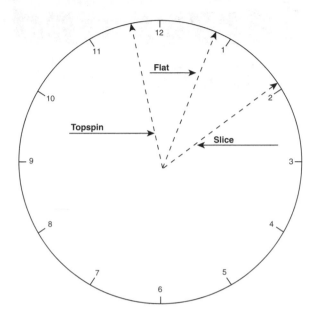

Before mastering the techniques of the most successful servers, players must first learn the fundamentals of the stroke, consistent placement, depth, spin, footwork, and power. The accuracy that comes from intense practice is a critical building block in perfecting any type of serve. Developing a successful serve will take many hours of repetitive practice, drilling, and playing enjoyable, pressure-free games. Because the serve is so important, players must spend as much time as they can to perfect it.

Description

The flat serve is the basic service motion. The setup for this serve is the foundation for the more advanced serves. When placed accurately, the flat serve often results in a service winner, a weak return, or an ace! The tradeoff is that it offers less control.

Execution

Players take a position at the baseline with the feet shoulder-width apart. The lead foot is at a 45-degree angle to the baseline, and the rear foot is parallel to it. The hands are relaxed and at waist level. Players hold the ball lightly in the left hand with the fingertips and use the eastern grip. With the ball facing up in the palm, players lower the arms, simultaneously taking the racket back and transferring weight to the rear foot. While reaching up to toss the ball, players continue to move the racket back. At the end of the backswing, they release the ball with the tossing arm fully extended and fingertips pointed upward. The face of the racket makes contact directly behind the ball. Right-handers strike the ball when the toss is in the one o'clock position. Left-handers use the eleven o'clock position. As the forward swing begins, body weight shifts forward. As players complete the weight transfer, they hit the ball while simultaneously rotating the shoulders and hips forward to add fluidity and power. To add speed, they accelerate the wrist by snapping through contact. Players follow through by hitting up and out, and then letting the racket head come down across the body to the left.

Tip

To establish a rhythm, players can say to themselves "Toss" when releasing the ball and "Hit" at contact.

Description

The slice serve gives players more spin and control than the flat serve does but less power. The bounce is low and curves away from the opponent in the same direction as the spin. Players hit the serve with the face of the racket making contact at the two o'clock position for right-handers and at ten o'clock for left-handers. The slice is produced by contacting the back side of the ball, in this case with the racket face moving from inside to outside on a diagonal path when viewed from behind. When the ball hits the court, it will kick to the left for a right-hander and will stay lower than a topspin or flat serve does.

Execution

Players position themselves in the flat-service position and mirror the steps they take when serving a flat serve. When hitting a slice serve, players make contact by hitting the top right section of the ball. They place the toss out in front and slightly to the right of the body at two o'clock (ten o'clock for left-handers). After striking the ball at its highest point, they complete the follow-through.

Tip

If players are having trouble defending against a slice or spin serve, check their court positioning when they're returning this slippery service style. Players may be standing too far to the left, nearest the service-line center (T) of the deuce service court, which opens them up to a serve sliced or spun wide to their forehand if they're right handed or their backhand if they're left handed. Unfortunately, many players don't spend enough time developing the serve, let alone a spin serve. This is the most important part of the total game. Players should devote more time to developing a solid spin serve, the shot that starts all points, games, and matches.

29 — KICK-SERVE TECHNIQUE

Description

This serve offers more net clearance and spin, which helps cut down on double faults and throws opponents off balance. The kick serve occurs when the racket face brushes the back of the ball with the wrist snapping out in a left-to-right motion (reverse for left-handers).

Execution

Players position themselves at the baseline in the flat-service position. This set-up mirrors the flat serve with a slight twist. The upswing and the contact point with the ball are different. Players brush up the back of the ball while snapping the wrist up and out in a left-to-right motion, if right-handed. The toss should be placed at twelve o'clock right above the head. This location offers enough net clearance, leaving a slight margin for error. Players should remember to continue the snapping-up or brushing-up motion after striking the ball to give the ball net clearance and the topspin that causes the ball to kick up and over the opponent's head.

Tip

There are all sorts of variations on backswings—from how low to drop the racket head to how high above the head players should stop the racket head from dropping. No matter what, players must have the correct timing and motion to serve successfully. Players should remain relaxed from the start of the serve through impact and the finish. If players tighten up at any point during the progression stages of the service motion, they are thwarting their potential energy up through the racket and into the ball. This equals no power into the serve. Players should think of their arms as loose spaghetti or whips when transferring potential energy up and out through the racket and into the ball.

Patrick Rafter

Skunky Kick Serve

© Sport The library

Age 30, height six-feet-one, weight 190 pounds, right-handed. Patrick Rafter counts on his kick serve to make his serve-and-volley game scream right into his opponent's face, "Catch me if you can!" Dubbed the tennis "supreme being" by millions of young women around the world, Rafter was born in Mount Isa, Queensland, Australia. Affectionately nicknamed "Skunky" or "Pat," he started playing tennis at age 5. After graduating from high school and turning pro in 1991, Patrick and his brother Geoff traveled around Europe playing the satellite tour for a few years before Patrick swept to his first Grand Slam victory in 1997 at the U.S. Open, defeating Greg Rusedski in four sets, 6-3, 6-2, 4-6, 7-5. In 1998 he won five top tournaments in a row before returning again to the United States to defend his title at the 1998 U.S. Open. Australia has produced some of the world's greatest tennis players, including Rod Laver, Ashley Cooper, Lew Hoad, Ken Roswall, Fred Stolle, John Newcombe, and Pat Cash, but Patrick "Skunky" Rafter has been celebrated as Australia's greatest singles player since John Newcombe.

One of the most unforgettable moments in Rafter's career occurred in 1997 when, after losing a tournament in France, he returned his appearance fee because he felt that he didn't do a good job. In his words, "I didn't do a good job, so why should I get paid for it?" Pat is one player who truly believes that his duty in life is to put in more than he takes out. Patrick is now retired, surfing and riding his moped around his home in Bermuda with his son.

Description

This serve is the basic flat serve with some powerful footwork. While tossing the ball and shifting body weight forward, players step up to the baseline with the back foot and launch up and into the ball with both legs together. This action helps generate a tremendously powerful serve.

Execution

Players take a position at the baseline or the service-line center (T) and start from the natural service ready position. They mirror the steps of the flat serve but after transferring body weight forward, they simultaneously step up with the back foot while tossing the ball, place the back foot next to the lead foot, bend both knees, and launch up and out with the legs together. This sequence produces tremendous power from the lower body. Players strike the ball at the peak of the toss for net clearance and control, and then land on the lead foot. They complete the follow-through and recover.

Tip

The accuracy of the toss is especially important when adding fancy footwork to the serve. After players toss the ball, it essentially stays stationary, but the body will be moving all over the place. Players must therefore place the toss in the same location every time they toss. They must practice tossing the ball at least as much as they practice serving the ball, if not more. A great way to learn how to hit up on the serve is by sitting or kneeling on the baseline or serviceline next to the center (T). This type of positioning forces a player to really extend the racket head up and into the ball before swinging out to the service court area. Players who crave more pace and depth on the serve should try exhaling to help prevent a choked stroke and smoothly accelerate up and through the ball.

31—SQUAT LAUNCH SERVE TECHNIQUE

Description

This aggressive service motion will add some hot pepper to the basic service motion. For players who prefer their weight under them and their feet close together, this is the serve. It is an explosive service style that allows players to utilize their lower body to the max during the service motion. This utilization of the lower body is what gives the squat launch serve its power.

Execution

This is a sweet addition to the basic service motion. Players follow the flat-service procedure but during the backswing of the racket, they bend the knees, launch off the balls of the feet, and hit the ball. They simultaneously toss the ball and bend the knees into a semi-crouching position. They begin the forward swing up to the ball and launch off the balls of both feet. At contact the body should be fully extended, the shoulders and hips should be rotated forward into the serve, and the feet should come up off the ground a couple of inches, not feet. Players land on the lead foot and complete the follow-through. This combination of steps creates an explosive serve, and is thus an excellent technique for any player to have in their repertoire.

Tip

No matter the style, the serve is the most elaborate stroke in tennis and the stroke that yields the greatest degree of personal differentiation. For the more advanced serving styles, players must learn to use their legs, hips, shoulders, trunk rotation, and wrist snap to generate powerful, aggressive serves. Players must also remember to serve with a target in mind – no blind serving. Players should become unpredictable servers by moving the ball around in the service boxes, keeping their head up, and watching their racket connect with the ball.

32—CROSSOVER LAUNCH SERVE TECHNIQUE

Description
This serve is the basic, or natural, flat-serve motion with fancy footwork to provide more spin, power, and superb placement. This serve requires good timing and balance.

Execution
Players position themselves at the baseline next to the center (T) and begin in the flat-service stance. Players begin the forward swing while bending the knees and simultaneously shifting body weight forward. After completing the weight transfer, they launch off the lead foot and strike the ball at the peak of the toss for maximum power and control. Players kick the lead foot back, scissor the rear foot forward, and then land on it. They bring the back leg forward as they contact the ball and complete the follow-through to recover.

Tip
The continental grip is the preferred grip for the crossover launch serve because it allows players to use racket-head speed more effectively and helps create the superspin that makes this serve unique.

33—FLAT SERVICE

Objective
This drill helps solidify the grip and footwork needed for the flat-service technique.

Description
Players learn how to create more speed and power using this flat-service technique.

Execution
To get more speed with the flat serve, players take a position a few feet behind the service line. They serve the ball into the service box using the flat-service grip (one o'clock for right-handers and eleven o'clock for left-handers) and the correct ball toss. Players practice increasing racket-head speed by accelerating up and into the ball and then out to the target that they have set up. Serves go to all target areas—down the center, down the middle, and into the far corner in both service boxes. The feet stay stationary except that the rear foot rises up onto the toes on and after contact with the ball. The face of the racket makes contact directly behind the ball. Players serve at targets using 75 percent power and complete the follow-through.

Tip
Tossing and balance are two essential ingredients for executing an effective serve, whatever the style.

34—SLICE SERVICE

Description
This drill helps players put a slice, or sidespin, on the ball. Like the flat power serve, the slice serve can be an offensive service weapon.

Execution
Players take a position at the service line and stand in the flat-serve position. Using the semicontinental grip, they toss the ball forward and a little to the right if right-handed, and turn the hitting shoulder away while transferring weight onto the lead (left) foot. They keep the hitting elbow higher than the hitting shoulder as the racket head falls deep into the throwing position. With weight shifted forward and the body held upward as the knees straighten, they throw the racket head edge on to the ball while pronating the wrist (turning the wrist and forearm together), shoulders, and hips simultaneously. Contact with the ball occurs at two o'clock, and the racket head accelerates on contact. The racket head, not the arm or elbow, must lead the downswing. Players must not toss the ball too far to the right when hitting slice serves because doing so will put too much spin and height on the ball. Players then complete the follow-through.

35—KICK SERVICE

Description
This drill helps players learn how to hit an effective kick serve. Once mastered, this serve is extremely reliable because the spin creates a dipping flight that allows high net clearance. This serve is also an offensive weapon that players can use for a first service.

Execution
Players position themselves on the service line standing in the flat-service stance. A few targets are set up anywhere inside one of the service boxes. Players toss between twelve and one o'clock to achieve proper balance with the kick serve. If players have poor balance during the serve, the toss will probably be too far to the left and behind them. They start the downward swing and rotate the hitting shoulder while tossing the ball. As their weight transfers forward onto the lead foot, both knees bend and the racket head simultaneously drops behind the head. Players thrust the body upward while throwing the racket head up and brushing up the back of the ball. They snap the wrist up and forward so that the racket face connects with the ball crisply. After completing the snap-up-and-across action, the racket leaves the ball and arcs up and out to the right as the rear foot swings across the service line. Players complete the follow-through with the racket coming down past the right side of the body. The back foot comes down inside the court. Those having trouble getting kick action on the ball should hit left to right with pronation, be sure to use the legs, and really accelerate the racket head.

36 — THRUST LAUNCH SERVICE

Objective
This drill helps players learn how to use their legs to create powerful serves.

Description
The thrust launch service motion is the basic flat-service motion with some fancy footwork to help create power.

Execution
Players start in the natural service position (flat-service position), standing on the service line and keeping the feet comfortably shoulder-width apart for maximum balance and a strong foundation. While tossing the ball and shifting weight forward, they step up to the service line with the rear foot and bend both knees because they must spring into this serve. Using the semicontinental grip, they whip the racket head through the ball. They sit with the toss and then launch up and into the ball with both legs together. This action will generate tremendous power. Players should first practice this footwork pattern without the ball and racket to get the feel and timing of the thrust launch.

Variation
Players should practice by positioning themselves at the baseline and slowly starting to coordinate the swing motion with the use of the legs so that the left foot lands well inside the baseline. Finally, they use the legs and incorporate racket-head speed with the thrust.

37 — SQUAT LAUNCH SERVICE

Objective
This drill helps players learn to use their legs, hips, shoulders, trunk rotation, and wrist snap to generate powerful serves.

Description
This service motion adds pepper to the basic service motion by allowing players to use the lower body to the max during the service motion.

Execution
This serve is all about precision, so practice should first occur without a racket or ball. Players take a position at the baseline center (T), starting in the natural or basic service stance. The lead foot should be at a 45-degree angle to the baseline, if right-handed, and the rear foot parallel to the baseline. The arms should be at waist level, with the ball held lightly with the fingertips in the tossing hand. Players simultaneously toss the ball and bend the knees into a squat position. They begin the forward swing up to the ball and launch off the balls of the feet. At contact, the body should be fully extended, and the shoulders and hip rotated into the serve. Players land on the lead foot and follow through.

38—CROSSOVER LAUNCH SERVICE

Objective

This drill will help players develop superb racket head speed, pronation of the forearm with a pronounced wrist-snapping action, and a better feel for using the continental forehand grip. Most important, though, it develops both the timing and the footwork rhythm needed to solidify the crossover service technique.

Description

The footwork is the most important part to this serve, and the recommended grip for intermediate and advanced players is the continental forehand grip.. Practicing the crossover footwork pattern from the service line helps develop the timing and footwork rhythm needed to make this advanced service motion more natural.

Execution

Players position themselves at the baseline and stand in the natural service stance (flat-serve position), using the continental forehand grip. While tossing the ball, players simultaneously begin the forward swing while shifting body weight forward. As they complete the weight transfer, they launch off the lead foot and hit the ball at the peak of the toss for maximum power. They kick the lead foot back, scissor the rear foot forward, and land on it. Players complete the follow-through and recover.

Variation

Players progress to the baseline and continue to serve to targeted areas within the service courts. They practice their second serves from the baseline, using less spin but never forgetting the launch movement. The second serve should be almost as effective as the first serve. Players should do as the pros do—serve big, first and second.

Tip

Players should avoid lowering the dominant arm too quickly or bringing the front foot up to the baseline too soon. This action results in faults, mis-hits, and loss of power. The dominant arm should stay up longer to ensure high net clearance. The back foot should come up to the baseline simultaneously with the toss, so that the hips and shoulders rotate smoothly and together. For maximum power, the dominant foot must land inside the baseline. Players should remember to complete the follow-through. This crucial tactic helps players recapture good balance and effectively get back into position and ready for the return of serve.

39—SERVICE REPETITION

Objective
This drill helps develop footwork, dexterity, coordination, and all service techniques.

Description
Practicing the serve is crucial, and repetition is the key to having a reliable, consistent serve. By doing a task repeatedly, players can make it become second nature. In this drill, players pick areas in the service box to serve to and vary the types of serves to each.

Execution
Players designate service boxes to which they will hit spin, flat, slice, and kick serves. The following service plan should be part of the tennis workout. Players should warm up and stretch, serving from the service line to warm up the shoulder properly. They should try to hit 25 spin, flat, slice, and kick serves to each half of each service box. They should serve down the center (T), down the middle, and into the left corner of the deuce service box and then switch service courts and repeat the drills. Players hit 100 serves to begin and increase the amount as their skill level rises.

40—SERVICE BREATHING

Objective
This drill helps create a fluid motion when striking the ball.

Description
Breathing is the key to promoting two good habits during any stroke. First, by breathing through the serve, players avoid the tendency to hold their breath, which can lead to overall tightness of the muscles in the arm, wrist, and elsewhere. Breathing helps relax the entire body, allowing more racket-head speed through contact and creating more power. Second, breathing during the point and taking deep breaths between points is the best way to combat the jitters players may feel under pressure.

Execution
Players can use this simple exercise while hitting ground strokes or serving. Every time they strike the ball they should exhale. While playing out a point, they try to focus on their breathing. Slow and steady breathing is best. The rhythm I use for my students is the bounce-breath technique. They say "bounce" to themselves when the ball bounces, and they breathe out loud when striking the ball. Monica Seles makes that sound when she's striking the ball.

41—SERVICE BALANCE

Objective

This drill helps players learn the importance of balance when serving.

Description

Without balance, players can't recover from hitting shots and will be unable to control weight transfer into serves, ground strokes, or volleys, or recover after hitting overheads. Loss of balance also hinders the learning process, which will cause frustration and loss of confidence.

Execution

Players take positions at the baseline or service-line center (T). They stand in the natural service stance (flat-service stance), begin the serve, and check to see if the racket arm is raised in a back-scratch position with the nonracket hand limp at the side. In this position the body is not in balance. Both arms should work together. Players should practice pushing upward with the nonracket hand after performing the ball toss. The racket should be raised and in the back-scratch position at the same time. This move will help keep the racket and players' head up and the body flowing together. Players should practice pointing or lifting up with the ball after tossing to hit a serve.

Variation

This exercise can be performed without the use of the tennis racket. Players who are right handed should pretend to salute the back of their head with the right hand. The right palm faces the back of the head and right elbow is lifted above the right shoulder, while simultaneously lifting the ball-tossing hand (left hand if right-handed) to get both arms working together. Players should then rotate their shoulders, trunk, and hips together and catch the tossed ball at the peak of the toss with their racket hand (right hand if right-handed).

Tip

Pointing at the tennis ball is one of the most important things players can do to improve the accuracy and balance of the serve and ground strokes. To maintain balance and keep momentum moving forward throughout the stroke, players should use the nonracket hand as the tracking and balancing hand. They keep it out in front of the body to track the incoming ball and push outward to move the body forward. They then follow through out to the target and into the non-racket hand and complete the follow-through. Players should also watch to ensure that their feet are shoulder-width apart. Most amateurs tend to stand with their feet too close together, resulting in poor balance and loss of power. Practicing the serve and chosen service style helps build the stroke and confidence needed to execute under competitive pressure. Practicing is the only way to make good technique permanent.

42—SERVICE GEOMETRIC

Objective
Visualization helps players see the court differently while drilling and learning to hit to specific areas on the court. Visualizing a pizza pie is an entertaining way to accomplish this task.

Description
While learning to direct the serve, players need to visualize the service boxes as quadrants, or many different slices in one box.

Execution
When serving into either service box, players should visualize the box as half of a large pepperoni pizza, with the pepperoni marking each target they want to aim for. To force the opponent out of court, players serve wide to the slice closest to the doubles alley. Or, to play it safe, they serve to the second slice, which gives more room for error within the service box. If the opponent is preparing to receive wide, players serve to slice number three, straight down the middle of the service box (T). Mmmm, that's good!

Tip
Players should remember that the follow-through is a natural continuation of the stroke. The racket should be moving toward the target area of the service box before its descent past the left side of the body (for right-handers).

43—WIDE SERVICE INTERCEPTION

Objective
This drill helps players train to move diagonally forward to return wide-hit serves.

Description
A serve hit into the corner of a service box will pull a player wide, off the court. This drill gets the feet moving in the correct direction so that players can counter the wide-hit serve and quickly recover to prepare for the return.

Execution
To return wide serves, players intercept the ball diagonally forward rather than sideways. By incorporating the ready-hop technique into the footwork, players will be able to move their feet diagonally forward to cut off the ball. When the opponent strikes the ball, players should be ready to attack the serve by giving a quick ready hop and a forward explosion into the ball at the same time. This move will cut down on the angle of the serve by taking it before it moves even wider. Taking the ball early also puts pressure on the opponent. The player's weight should be moving forward rather than sideways, thus giving more power with little or no extra effort.

44—KNUCKLE BALL

Objective
This simple drill helps players isolate the most important part of consistent serving—the toss and release.

Description
This tossing drill came by way of former baseball fanatic turned tennis fiend. She suggested to one young girl who kept tossing balls behind her head to hold onto the ball with her fingertips to produce a smooth, fluid motion. By focusing on the fingertips and holding lightly onto the ball, she stopped using her fingers to manipulate the ball and toss behind her.

Execution
Upon releasing the ball, players should imagine that their fingers are a gentle water fountain spouting up and out at the height of the extension. They gently hold the ball in the tossing hand and lift up the tossing arm. At full extension they release the ball with the fingertips and hand, palm up. If they curl the fingers or hand while tossing, they will toss the ball behind the head. For maximum net clearance and control, players should remember to focus on the ball and keep the head up when tossing and hitting. Trying to sneak a peek at the serve will cause the head to drop too soon, resulting in a mis-hit.

45—SERVICE FOOTWORK

Objective
This drill helps players release the rear foot more naturally, improving the rhythm of the weight transfer needed for good serving.

Description
The throwing motion used in playing catch mimics the serving motion. When throwing a ball to acquire depth, the release is higher. Likewise, to get more height and depth with the serve, players must swing up and hit out using the same throwing motion.

Execution
Players position the feet in the natural service position, shoulder-width apart. In throwing a ball to a partner, they will notice that the rear foot wants to come forward with the body. They should go ahead and let the back foot come around, transferring their weight toward the target. By tossing the ball out in front and making contact with the hitting arm fully extended, they can bring the back foot around into the court after contact, naturally transferring body weight toward the target.

Tip
Rhythm isn't just for singing and dancing; players need it for the serve, too.

46—SERVICE MOTION

Objective
This drill will help players acquire the fluidity needed for good serving.

Description
When serving, a fluid motion coupled with a high arc on the ball is important. A choppy service motion causes loss of power, poor placement, and lack of control.

Execution
Players begin developing the service by practicing throwing the ball into the opponent's service box. Either service box will do while players are standing on the service line. After achieving a reasonably high arc of clearance, players work their way back toward the baseline and notice the smooth, fluid rhythm they need to toss higher so that they can get the arc necessary for maximum net clearance. When they are ready to practice the service motion, they start with the racket already in completion of half of the backswing. They start with the arm and racket above the dominant shoulder, the right shoulder if right-handed, with the top of the racket head pointing toward the sky. They toss the ball and accelerate the racket head up and out on contact. After striking the ball, the lead foot should follow through naturally past the baseline. Making the ball and racket dance together is tough in the beginning, but practice will develop a more rhythmic feeling. Players should practice the full-swing motion first from the service line and slowly work their way back toward the baseline.

47—SERVICE TOSSING

Objective
This drill isolates the service toss, the most crucial part of the serve.

Description
The success of the serve is directly related to the toss. A low toss can result in loss of power and little, if any, net clearance. Many players feel as though a high toss causes loss of control, so they must practice this drill to obtain proper height.

Execution
Players hold the ball lightly in the fingers and smoothly move the arm downward and upward. They release the ball when the arm is at full extension, with the fingertips pointing upward. The tossing arm should stay up a fraction after releasing the ball. Letting the tossing arm collapse too quickly after the toss can result in loss of power and short serves into the net. Players should practice the three types of tosses—topspin, slice, and flat—and try to use them during practice matches and real match play.

chapter 5

Lobs and Overheads

It's been a long, lonely road over the years for the underused lob. Used primarily in a defensive situation, such as recovering when forced out of position or when under attack from a net rusher, it was seen only as a reply to an overhead smash hit by an opponent.

Today the lob and overhead are weapons to be reckoned with. Lobs and overheads are no longer primarily doubles shots, and singles players are using both shots to put tremendous pressure on servers, volleyers, pushers, and the baseline counterpunchers. Because of this, players must not neglect to drill the lob and overhead. They need to learn where and when to use the lob and how to build up points to set up the opponent for a devastating smash.

By practicing both strokes in gamelike situations, players will develop the confidence to use these master strokes whenever they need an easy point or need to throw off the opponent's game. Lobbing and hitting overheads can be a lot of fun, especially when players know when and how to perform the strokes. This section on lobbing and smashing will help players develop tactics to use when building the perfect game plan for their style of game.

48—TOPSPIN FOREHAND LOB TECHNIQUE

Description

Hit properly, the topspin lob can be the most devastating stroke in tennis. It is usually a winner every time it is hit. Once it clears the racket and hits the court, it's virtually impossible for an opponent to run down the ball. By mixing up passing shots and topspin lobs, players will keep even the best net rushers guessing and off balance.

Execution

To hit an effective lob, the racket must make an extreme low-to-high motion and meet the ball in front of the body. The follow-through should finish behind the ear on the racket side of the head. This swing will generate the spin that's necessary to bring the ball down quickly once it clears the volleyer. The racket face should be slightly open with the bottom edge of the frame just in front of the top edge. Players should tilt the shoulders back a bit to ensure that the ball gets the necessary height. Generating topspin with a slightly open racket face works because this low-to-high motion is so pronounced.

Tip

A good topspin lob will come in handy on many occasions, but it's most effective when the opponent is serving and volleying or after the opponent makes an approach shot. The golden key to successful lobbing is how to properly disguise the stroke. Players should set up to hit the lob exactly as they would for any ground stroke, and remember to use this calculated shot sparingly. If players overuse this strategic shot their opponents will be more adept at reading when they are about to unleash this shot, and will be better prepared to run down the lob and counter-punch the attack.

49—BACKHAND LOB TECHNIQUE

Description

The backhand lob can be effectively hit with either a one-handed or two-handed backhand. The two-handed backhand topspin lob is particularly effective because it's almost impossible to read. Although two-handed players are usually more effective at disguising the lob, one-handers can also be successful with this shot. One-handers can use the same routine in practicing their backhand lob as they do with the forehand, but they need to pay closer attention to the way they hold the racket.

Execution

Players with one-handed backhands don't seem to be as willing to hit topspin lobs as players who use two hands are. For a one-handed lob, the grip must be a full continental backhand grip. The more exaggerated the grip and the more players roll the hand away from the forehand grip, the easier it will be to hit with topspin. After making an exaggerated low-to-high swing, players should finish the long follow-through next to the ear on the dominant side of the body. As with the forehand, players should tilt the shoulders back and open the racket face slightly while making contact. This action will get the ball in the air quickly. For a two-handed lob, the preparation and the way players hold the racket in making the swing should be identical to what they use for the regular ground stroke. Although the low-to-high motion will be more exaggerated, players should finish in nearly the same follow-through position as they would on a backhand ground stroke.

Tip

Disguising the lob is key. The preparation should mirror the preparation for the passing shot. At the last moment the player hits up to give extra lift.

50—RIGHT EAR, LEFT EAR

Objective

This drill helps players generate maximum topspin with the forehand and backhand lobbing technique.

Description

Players get the feel of the quick, wristy motion they need to hit this shot.

Execution

With racket and ball in hand up at the net, players attempt with the racket strings to press the ball against the net strap and brush straight up the back of the ball. The follow-through should stay on the same side of the stroke. For right-handers hitting a forehand lob, the follow-through continues past the right ear. For the backhand lob, the follow-through continues past the left ear. The quick-snapping brushing-up motion will make the ball spin forward with tremendous velocity.

Variation

Players hold a ball several inches from the net strap and bounce it on the ground. As it reaches net height, they make the identical brushing motion and follow-through. Next, they back up a few steps, open up the racket face slightly, and repeat the motion and follow-through. The ball should have plenty of topspin and clear the net by 10 feet. Players hit a topspin lob off a volley from a partner, attempting to clear the net player's outstretched racket by at least 10 feet.

51—DEEP LOB

Objective

This drill helps players learn how to lob high over any opponent.

Description

The deep lob is also called the point-saving lob or defensive lob. There are two types of lobs—the defensive lob and the powerful offensive lob. This drill focuses on making them interchangeable.

Execution

Player A stands four feet behind the service line and feeds balls to player B at the opposite baseline. After hitting to player B, player A extends the racket overhead. Player B then tries to lob over the outstretched racket but within the boundaries of the court. Player A may move laterally but not backward. If player A is able to touch the ball, or if the ball is out, he or she wins the point. If player B hits the lob over player A and in the court, he or she wins the point. The players switch after 15 points.

52—DROP AND LOB

Objective
This drill helps players learn to lob an opponent after he or she tries a drop shot.

Description
Doing this drill repeatedly in a match can cause an opponent to fall apart. By using a drop shot and then a lob, players can force the opponent to sprint forward and try to hit an effective return and then backward to try to hit another. With the opponent then out of steam, the player should be able to hit an easy winner.

Execution
Players position themselves at opposite ends of the court on the baseline and begin rallying. Player A hits a drop shot on player B, who attempts to recover the drop shot and hit a lob over player A. They repeat this sequence 10 times and then switch positions.

Variation
This drill can be done on the minicourt area by instituting the lob volley. Players A and B are opposite each other on the service line. Player A hits a drop shot to player B. Player B moves forward and returns the shot with another drop shot. Player A moves forward and hits a lob volley over player B's head. They repeat this 10 times and switch positions.

53—LOB AND PASS

Objective
This drill helps players learn how to respond and recover after failing to hit a lob high enough over the opponent.

Description
This drill helps players recover from a poorly executed lob attempt while placing them in a gamelike situation.

Execution
Player A is positioned at the net, and player B is on the baseline of the opposite side of the court. Player B hits the ball to A, who must hit it back to player B, who, in turn, must hit a lob. Player A attempts to put the overhead away, and player B then tries to win the point with lobs or passing shots from the backcourt. They play 15 points and then switch.

Tip
Players must not let the ball drop too low. The higher they make contact, the less likely they are to hit into the net. Players should always track the ball with the free hand.

54 — OVERHEAD LOB TECHNIQUE

Description

The first component of an effective overhead is recognizing and reacting quickly to the opponent's lob. Studying the techniques of Tim Henman's overhead has helped my game, and my students' games, reach new levels. The basic strategy of the overhead is to win the point outright. Players can do this by simply overpowering the ball or by executing with precision.

Execution

Players establish a solid position at the net and hold the racket with a continental grip. An advantage of using the continental grip when volleying is that when lobbed, players don't have to change the grip to hit the overhead. When the ball approaches, players drop the right foot back and begin to turn the hips and shoulders sideways. After completing the body rotation, players should be at a 90-degree angle to the net. By turning sideways when hitting an overhead, players can uncoil, rotate the hips and shoulders, and then make a smooth, powerful swing. Keeping the feet close together will allow a quick jump up to the ball. When leaving the ground and exploding upward, players focus on the ball and start to bring the right arm up to make the swing. At this point players start to rotate the shoulders. The position of the racket and body closely resemble the position used in the serving motion. Players must keep the ball slightly to the dominant side (in the two o'clock position). With the ball high above the head, they keep the arm loose and the grip relaxed so that the wrist can snap at contact. The wrist snap generates racket-head speed and brings the ball down into the court.

55 — OVERHEAD SMASH TECHNIQUE

Objective

This drill helps players establish good rhythm for hitting effective overheads.

Description

This drill helps players learn the techniques needed to hit consistent, effective offensive overheads.

Execution

Players line up on the side of the court near the net post. One at a time, they sidestep out to the middle of the court, touch the net with the racket, and shuffle backward for an overhead hit by a server. After successfully hitting the overhead, they must close back in to the net, touch the net, and hit a second overhead. As the hitters develop more confidence and a good rhythm, they use oscillation and deeper overheads, gradually moving into randomly directed overheads. Hitters should always return to home base with a good split step or ready hop. Players should repeat this drill often to develop confidence and good footwork for hitting overheads.

Tactics and Strategy

To play aggressive singles or doubles, players must keep their cool. They must never let their opponents see them sweat, and they should take total control of every point. Players take balls out onto the court, spin the racket to decide who serves, and commit to every shot they plan—all without hesitation or choking. Players must take advantage of every opportunity to attack the net and capitalize on the opponent's mistakes. They must be prepared to counterattack when the tide turns against them. But how do they do it? What type of strategic game plan will work best? What is a game plan? Brad Gilbert summed it up for James Blake by helping him realize that "every player has a style, and every style has a weakness." The next few chapters explain how to develop a game plan for singles or doubles play. Players learn how to play offensive and defensive tennis and practice the drills that will help them hone a signature style of play so that they will never again be caught off guard. People never enter a sales meeting without a plan of action, so why would they play a partner, club match, or tournament match without one?

chapter 6

Offensive Play

The strategies available to tennis players today are boundless. With new techniques of play and new equipment, players need to make stronger, more aggressive plans of action. Before stepping onto the court, they must have a game plan in mind—a signature winning strategy designed specifically for them. A plan can be as simple as hitting a three-to-one combination of three shots to the opponent's backhand and then spanking a forehand crosscourt to attack the net, or as complex as coming in on every third service point and attacking a certain area of the court. Players should include in their plan ways of building up the points to use their strengths, specific style of play, mental approach, and physical conditioning. Every match should be planned from beginning to end. The plan should include how they will defend against certain game styles, what shots they will use, and what they will think about at changeovers. In developing a master game plan, players should take into account the different styles of games they will encounter during competition.

Mr. Server himself, Stan Smith, believes that different attack methods work best against particular styles of play:

- **The Sloth.** The slothful player is likely to have difficulty reaching the wide-breaking serve, so players should put more spin on the slice serve. This type of player hates to move, so players should really try to move him or her around. The crosscourt down-the-line pattern or drop shot–lob pattern can be effective. Whatever the pattern, players should be patient and remember that the sloth is a slow mover. Rushing their own play will only cause unforced errors.

- **Speedy Gonzalez.** Variety is the key here. Players should keep this kind of player off balance by mixing up placement and spin types. Speedy will overrun balls, trip over his or her own two feet, and hit crazy, unpredictable shots. Players should keep this kind of opponent guessing and periodically throw in some soft stuff. An effective tactic is the three-to-one pattern—three shots to one side and then a step in to hit the fourth in the opposite direction. Players can run this pattern until the opponent faints from exhaustion.

- **The Hulk.** This type of player usually has slow reflexes because of big, bulky muscles. Players can try flat, hard serves or slice right into his or her body. This player can't move well so any combination of shots hit far enough away should do the trick.

Players should develop game plans to deal with the styles of all these kinds of players. The stronger a player's game and game plan, the more likely he or she is to succeed in upcoming matches. Players should be aware of their strengths and weaknesses and plan their strategy accordingly.

In the game of tennis, winning depends not only on how well a player performs but also on how well he or she customizes a strategy and overall approach to the opponent. Five basic offensive shots should be kept in mind when developing a game plan. By developing each of these shots, players will have a package of offensive strengths with which to build an overall offensive game plan.

- **Crosscourt shot.** To get the opponent moving right away, players should start the point with a crosscourt shot. The opponent will have to run more because a crosscourt shot can be hit at greater angles. The more the opponent must run for a ball, the less chance he or she has to get set and transfer weight into the shot and the greater the chance of a weak return. By hitting to a strength with a crosscourt shot, players may expose a weakness to the other side on the next shot. By returning the ball crosscourt when out of position, players will have four or five fewer recovery steps to take to get back to home base.

  Players should remember that the racket face controls the direction of shots. The ball will always go in the direction that the strings are facing because the ball bounces off the racket at right angles. For example, when the racket face is facing diagonally across the net, the ball will go crosscourt. When the racket face is facing squarely at the net with the strings parallel to the net, the ball will go down the line.

- **Down-the-line shot.** The opponent who hits down the line will have to move a considerable distance to get to a crosscourt return. If the player can return the down-the-line shot with an aggressive crosscourt, he or she has an excellent chance to win the point outright.

  On the down-the-line shot the ball travels a shorter distance and over a higher part of the net than it does with the crosscourt shot, so players must allow more leeway for error. They should hit this shot to change the routine of the basic crosscourt pattern, to hit at the opponent's weakness, or to hit behind an opponent who is running fast to cover the opposite side of the court.

- **Short shot.** The opponent who has an aversion to approaching the net probably suffers from "net jitters." Players can take advantage of this opportunity by hitting a short shot to draw the opponent in to the net. Players may also want to return short if the opponent is pulling them up to the net and lobbing over their heads or aggressively passing them. Players who are not effective when pulled up to the net may want to bring the opponent to the net first by using a soft, short ball instead of an approach shot. When the opponent hits a short ball (weak shot) and players must move into the midcourt offensive zone to return it, they can play it as a drop shot, which tends to pull the opponent up and out of position. In addition, short shots following high floaters can be effective change-of-pace shots.

- **Passing shot.** The most important principle in the use of passing shots is keeping the ball low so that the net rusher will be forced to hit it up, decreasing the opportunity to make an aggressive volley. Topspin balls drop faster than flat or underspin balls do. Therefore, players should know that most passing shots hit with substantial topspin are effective.

- **Drop shot.** Players who are comfortable with all the preceding shots have collected a formidable set of weapons of court destruction. Now they should learn to use one of the smallest yet most powerful shots in tennis. The drop shot can be extremely effective when playing against a base-liner who refuses to come up to the net, or off a return of serve (second serve) as long as the server habitually stays back. Players can also try it off a short ball that the opponent hits to them. Normally, players return deep, which is what the opponent expects, so the drop shot can catch him or her by surprise. The drop can also work well off the opponent's drop shot, as long as he or she is reasonably far back or off balance. If the drop shot is not a surprise, it won't work.

The drills in this chapter will help players build on their strengths and clean up some of their weaknesses so that their offensive game plan can take them to the finals of many tournaments to come.

56—FAST SWING

Objective

This drill helps players create a shortened backswing and tremendous racket-head speed for maximum power and control.

Description

To create lots of topspin with tremendous power, players must shorten the backswing to catch the ball earlier and farther out in front of the body.

Execution

Players begin with the racket head back as though they are about to hit a forehand. The grip should be in the semiwestern or full western grip. The wrist should be loose, but the grip should be tight. Players should practice whipping the racket head and snapping the wrist up and out through the hitting zone as fast as they can until they become accustomed to the feel and the motion has become fluid. Now they start rotating the upper body, the trunk, and the hips with the swing. Rotating the upper body smoothes out the stroke, allows an early catch of the ball, and creates tremendous momentum into the stroke.

57—BALL FEEDING

Objective

This drill is a fantastic way for players to learn how to shorten the backswing and create racket-head speed with control.

Description

Players who have watched teaching pros feed the ball have probably noticed that they seem to be able to do it all day without their arms falling off. They can perform the feed almost forever because they use a shortened backswing, trunk rotation, and fluid stroking. Feeding balls is a great way to get the feel of the fast, shortened movement of the racket head.

Execution

Players take a ball hopper onto the court and practice feeding to a partner, alternating between topspin, slice, and backspin and sending balls to different targets. They start by setting up cones or markers across the service line, and they try to hit each cone using all types of spin. They continue until they're accurately hitting most of the cones. The harder they hit, the shorter the backswing will become.

Variation

Once players are comfortable feeding to one player, they add more players and try to keep them moving and hitting without allowing them to stop. Players who can rhythmically feed several other players are on their way to racket-head speed perfection!

58—MINICOURT

Objective

This is an excellent drill to help players learn how to control the ball, feel the ball, shorten their steps, and learn the short backswing it takes to create power and even more control.

Description

If players have trouble controlling the pace of the ball or are unable to keep the ball in play within the boundaries of the mini-court area, then they will likely not be able to sustain a full-court rally. Players must learn to develop the muscle control it takes to change the spin and speed of the oncoming and outgoing ball. People say that Monica Seles did this drill for an hour at a time when she was training at the Bollettieri Tennis Academy. This drill is one of the best ways to develop good ball sense, racket-head speed, confidence, and effective trunk and hip rotation.

Execution

Players are positioned on opposite service lines. They try to stay at least two feet back from the service-line area so that they'll have room to step into the ball. Players should have about the same ability. They try to hit the ball back and forth, keeping it inside the service-court area. To keep the ball in play, players will notice that they must shorten the backswing, get underneath the ball, and use a tight brushing-up motion on the ball. If they try to use all arm with no racket-head speed, the ball will hit either the net or the curtain on the opposite side of the court.

Variation

Players should first work on consistency so they should try to keep at least 25 balls in play. Players should then focus on placement by hitting consistent crosscourt shots. After players can keep 25 or more crosscourt shots in play, they should try to hit only down the line consistently for 25 or more shots. Once players build confidence and gain good ball sense, they should try a combination of the crosscourt and down the line rally within the mini-court area only. Players should practice this exercise until they can maintain any set of rally combinations with confidence, consistency, and control. They then progress up to playing points, games, and then an entire match.

Tip

This drill isn't for the unconditioned player. Players must be in good shape to execute this drill effectively and play the games within this area. For conditioning drills, see part four beginning on page 175.

Serena Williams

The Princess of Serendip

© Sport The Library

Born September 26, 1981, height five-feet-10, weight 145 pounds, plays right-handed with a two-handed backhand, 15 career titles. Serena turned pro in 1995 under the thunderous strength of her mother and the superb strategic training of her coach, her father. Serena has taken over the number-2 spot on the WTA ranking computer, just one notch under her sister Venus. In 1997, ranked 304th in the world and very green in her professional career, Serena defeated two top-10 players at the 1997 Chicago Open and became the lowest-ranked player to defeat a top-5 player. She catapulted to the 102nd spot on the WTA computer. In 1998 her ranking rose to 53rd, and she became the third-highest-ranked player after only three major-tour, main-draw events since 1976. In 1999 Serena had a 16-match winning streak that included a player's first title, the longest since Steffi Graf's 23-match streak in 1986. Serena began the year 2000 by winning the Faber Grand Prix and ended the season by winning a gold medal at the Sydney 2000 Summer Olympics with her big sister in doubles. In 2001 Serena won her first title of the year at Indian Wells and finished the year by becoming the first player to win the WTA tour's season-ending championships in her debut. Serena won her second Grand Slam title at the French Open by defeating her sister Venus 7-5, 6-3 in the finals. The Williams sisters' success in Paris made them the two top-ranked players in the world (Venus number 1 and Serena number 2), a first for siblings. Congratulations!

59—INSIDE-OUT FOREHAND

Objective
Hitting this aggressive shot takes exquisite footwork, loads of confidence, and perfect timing.

Description
The inside-out forehand is a spectacularly devastating shot when hit correctly at the perfect time. This drill helps develop the footwork players need to run around the backhand and hit the inside-out forehand.

Execution
The drill begins with a ball fed out wide by a partner to the forehand. The player takes a position at the center baseline (T). Starting from that position, the player hits the ball down the line with heavy topspin. The next feed is to the backhand side but a little closer to the center T and just inside the baseline. Of course, the opponent will think, "Aha! My opponent is going to hit a backhand." But alas! The player runs around the backhand and hits an inside-out forehand into the backhand side of the court on the opposite side.

60—SPANK THAT BACKHAND

Objective
This drill isolates a killer tactical pattern. The drill helps players develop an aggressive pattern to add to the game plan.

Description
This drill specifically addresses how to use the backhand as a weapon. By setting up patterns for delivering every shot, players can dictate when to unleash the backhand to finish off the point.

Execution
A partner takes a position on the opposite side of the net and starts by feeding balls to the backhand side of the court. The player begins by hitting a few inside-out forehands. The next feed is to the backhand, closer to the center and a little inside of the baseline. This time the player steps into the ball and spanks a backhand down the line. This pattern helps the player open up the court by forcing the opponent to run wider and wider to retrieve the inside-out forehands. Once the court is opened up enough, the player can smack a backhand for the win or run around the backhand and spank a forehand up the line.

Tip
Players should practice footwork drills to master the athletic dexterity it takes to run around shots, hit sharp angles, and recover.

chapter 7

Defensive Play

My coach, my father, my biggest fan had only two things to say before every match I played: "Have a purpose and a plan in mind for every ball you hit." Defensive combat in a tennis match is a combination of good strategy, lots of heart, and tremendous effort. Players must be able to take advantage of their strengths when things seem to go awry by creating a defensive game plan that will allow them to make the most out of all their strokes and tennis know how. The more information that players can gather about an opponent's capabilities, the easier it will be for them to select a strategic defensive game plan to attack the opponent's weaknesses.

Players must remember, however, that strategy or game plans must be flexible. In many cases, the plan of action for winning may be correct, but the chosen strategy will fail to realize the goal. In that case, players must be able to recognize how the opponent is successfully counterattacking their game, and they must be willing to change their defensive game plan to meet the new circumstances. The drills in this section provide some alternative actions for the defensive game plan to help get players back onto the road of playing their game. My motto: "Where there's a will, there's a way!"

61—CONCENTRATE AND PLAY GREAT

Objective

This drill helps players identify that they are playing the ball, not their opponent. It also helps players understand the concept of "being the ball."

Description

The power of the mind is apparent at each stage of a tennis player's development. When players stop trying to beat their opponents and just stick to their game plans, they can play better tennis. Learning how to be the ball helps create a barrier in the mind and on the battlefield, the court. By being the ball, players can't and won't be persuaded to play their opponent's game.

Execution

Players should concentrate solely on the ball from the serve to the conclusion of the point, to the degree that the background from where it came will be blurred or unseen. They should not look for the opponent when hitting a passing shot. They should watch the ball before, during, and after the bounce and right into the racket strings. Players should hit the ball better than required to win the point, and they must remember to consider the spin and pace of the approaching ball. This strategy separates the players who win from those who won't. When players are rallying from the baseline, topspin gives the best control and leeway for safety. Intense spin means less pace. The less the spin, the greater the potential pace. Varying the spin is best. Players play 11-point games and incorporate the preceding strategy.

Variation

Players can add this time-tested concentration trick to the drill. While returning serve, players should focus on straightening out the strings in their racket. They should watch their opponent's ball toss, and when he strikes the ball say, "Hit." When the ball bounces in the players' service court, they can say, "Bounce," and when they hit the ball say, "Hit." The bounce-hit tactic can be used with every stroke and is a fantastic tool for keeping the eyes and mind focused on the action at hand instead of on what happened two shots ago.

Tip

As players gain experience, they learn to anticipate what type of return shot to expect from most opponents. Concentration equals smarter anticipation and smarter shot selection. Players should be patient and build points up to hit winners. Ten or 15 shots may be required before players get to the one that has their signature on it. Learning to read the opponent's body and racket position will help players identify different types of shots and ball spin.

Venus Williams

The Peaceful Power of Women's Tennis

© Human Kinetics

Venus started her tennis career at age 4 1/2. Her father coached her on neighborhood tennis courts. She turned pro on October 31, the eve of All Saints' Day, in 1994. Once Venus starting knocking on the WTA door of professional tennis, she stepped right in, fit right in, took over the game, and raised the bar of women's tennis forever. Venus became the first unseeded woman to make a United States Open final, and in 1998 she beat WTA number-one-ranked Martina Hingis at Sydney. She went on to win the first set off Lindsey Davenport at the Australian Open in 18 minutes, although later losing in three sets (1-6, 6-2, 6-3). She came back three weeks later, however, and claimed her revenge—braids, beads, and all—to beat Davenport (6-7, 6-2, 6-3) for the first time and win her first singles title. In 2000 Venus became one of the top players in history after winning two consecutive Grand Slams (Wimbledon and the U.S. Open) in a 26-match winning streak. *Sports Illustrated* gave her the 2000 Spokeswoman of the Year award. Ghetto Cinderella? I don't think so!

62—WINDY DAY, NO PROBLEM

Objective
This drill helps players learn how to play effectively on windy days.

Description
It's been said that windy day tennis is the great leveler of different ability levels. On a windy playing day a lesser-skilled player and a higher-skilled player may appear to be equal unless one of the two players learns how to use the wind to their advantage. The secret to playing on a windy day is players shouldn't fight it – they should let the wind work for them, not against them. Whether playing with the wind behind them or in a crosswind, players must alter their playing style to be successful. By using the wind to their advantage, players can throw their opponents off track, who are already thrown off by the wind.

Execution
When the wind is with the player (at the back of the player), his or her shots go deep while the opponent's shots are shorter. Players can be more aggressive in going to the net. When serving and volleying, they can attack second serves and go to the net. Using the offensive lob and following it to the net or using the defensive lob crosscourt adds to the margin for error. Players should anticipate shorter, slower shots from the opponent, especially on lobs, slices, and drop shots.

When the wind is against the players, their shots will tend to fall short. Players should try to hit the ball a little harder than normal to keep the ball deep. They can use drop shots for an element of surprise, and they should avoid the lob, which may land short and produce an easy put-away for the opponent. A crosswind can dramatically change the path of the ball so players must concentrate on their footwork and get into proper position for each shot. Finally, players must adjust the aim of their shots (left or right) to compensate for the crosswind.

Tip
On gusty days players should let high-hit lobs or overheads bounce before attempting to hit them. The wind will cause the ball to take all sorts of frustrating twists and turns before they attempt to hit their desired shot. Serving also can be extremely frustrating on windy days. Patience, dexterity, and a mind of steel are just a few of the ingredients needed to tackle serving and hitting ground strokes on windy days. Players must modify the service toss when playing on windy days. Crosswinds will blow the toss sideways, winds from behind will blow the toss forward, and winds from ahead will blow the toss right back at the player.

63 — SUNNY DAYS AGAIN

Objective
This drill helps players learn how to adapt to playing on bright, sunny days.

Description
Trying to serve or hit an overhead when looking directly into the sun can be painful and frustrating. But methods are available for players to use on those beautiful sunny days so that they can get a tan and still play an enjoyable game of tennis.

Execution
If the sun is directly overhead when players are trying to serve, they must alter the toss. They can try moving the position of the toss until they can see it, or they can toss slightly lower. When deciding who will serve or receive first and the opponent chooses to serve first, players should allow the opponent to serve first on the shady side so that they will have to serve only one game in the sun and can serve the second in the shade. When receiving an overhead, players should let it bounce. Players in control of the ball and on the shady side of the court should hit lots of lobs and attack the net often.

Tip
Players shouldn't complain about bad weather, remembering that conditions are the same on both sides of the court.

64 — TIEBREAKER

Objective
This drill helps players fight for that last game when the match is tied.

Description
When players are faced with either winning or losing a match because the score is tied, they must play a 12-point tiebreaker. This drill helps players develop the fortitude it takes to compete in a pressured game situation.

Execution
Players must play points following the standard USTA-approved 12-point tiebreaker format. Players take positions and play a regular tennis match. Player A serves the first point into the deuce court. Player B starts the sequence of two serves per point. Player B serves the second point into the advantage court and the next point into the deuce court. The next two serves go to player A, who starts the next serve into the advantage court. When the players reach the sixth point, they switch sides. No rest period occurs during tiebreaker play. The player who reaches 7 points wins the game and the set. Note that the player who serves the last point of one of the 6-point segments serves the first point of the next one from the deuce court. Players should practice this method until they are comfortable when playing close matches.

65—CHOKE SYNDROME

Objective
This drill helps players develop a plan of attack when their nerves try to take over a match.

Description
Choking on court happens even to the best players. Building psychological strength is crucial to avoiding choking. When players choke, they may become so nervous in the middle of a match that they can't breathe, let alone hit a little yellow ball over that gigantic net. Breathing helps players relax their nerves or anxiety and it allows their body to work synchronistically, so they can focus on the game instead of their fear. Players who feel that fear should try this exercise to help them relax the next time they feel as if they are about to play Pete or Andre.

Execution
By incorporating these tactical moves, players can conquer the opponent and feel as if they're the king or queen of the court again. They should try to focus only on the ball, not the opponent, and make a conscious effort to breathe out or grunt every time they hit the ball. By using that method, they will find it almost impossible to play a short, jerky stroke that will cause them to lose control over their shots. A choked stroke results from the choppy stroke that players use when they suck in their breath. Players should breathe out as they swing and continue until they have followed through. If players feel that things seem to be spinning out of control, they should stop themselves and take a moment to collect their thoughts. They should think about their game plan, what they can do to alter it, and then just do it. The choke syndrome should vanish, and players will be on their way to playing to the best of their ability.

Tip
Here are a few tactical tricks players can incorporate into their game plan. Players should focus their nervous energy into getting more of their first serves in. They should recognize and accept their prematch jitters, then move on from there. They should also never let the opposition see them sweat. They should keep their on-court composure and play one point at a time. They should never look one point back or one point ahead, just play the point they're faced with at the moment. Finally, players should stick with the game plan but be flexible enough to adjust it if they must. People rarely play the way they warm up, so players should laugh off the attempted psyche job.

66 — CHANGEOVER

Objective

This exercise helps players develop a private set of crucial techniques to keep on court during match play. They can think of it as their secret pocket tennis coach.

Description

When playing tournaments or club matches, players are entitled to take 90 seconds to rest between games and after every odd game. They should spend this time wisely by focusing on the game plan and preparing for the next move.

Execution

Players should never rush to get back into the fire just because the opponent is standing ready to serve. The opponent's action is a tactical maneuver to throw off the player's rhythm. If things aren't going well, players should take this time to think back over the last game. Is the serve working? Are returns going deep and to the targeted areas? Players should check the game plan. Are they sticking to what works for them? They should avoid thinking too much and concentrate only on the last game and the game plan. They should stick with the game plan but be flexible at the same time. Perhaps a player goes into a match knowing that the opponent has a weak forehand but quickly finds that the opponent is winning big with it. The opponent's forehand has become an effective weapon, and the player must change his or her plan.

Tip

Advanced planning can really pay off in doubles, so players should be sure to plan. When they sit down during changeovers, players should talk quietly with their partners about strategy. Two heads are often better than one.

chapter 8

Equalizing Game Styles

Players must recognize that they have a style, that the opponent has a style, and that nothing can or should be done about it. So players should play their game and understand that they are never as good at other styles as they are at their own. When the game plan starts to break down, players should make only minor adjustments to their style without changing it entirely. Every tennis competitor will meet players who use different tactics to try to win. Players should take a close look at the various game styles and tactics they can use to counter each. By incorporating some of the tools they learn into the game plan, players can prepare to play and counter almost any style of play.

Players will learn how to counterbalance or equalize styles of play by making small changes in their game plan so that they will be able to stick with their style of play. They will also learn how to balance game styles of different ability levels by using different methods of scoring and game handicapping. This chapter introduces several tactical maneuvers to help players become better and smarter competitors.

67—COURT HANDICAP

Objective
This strategy helps equalize different ability levels so that players can compete against each other.

Description
A stronger player can get a great workout by playing half-court and full-court tennis with less skilled players. Conversely, a weaker player can learn a lot by playing against a stronger player. By using this method, two unequal players can be equal.

Execution
The stronger player or players (A) play into the midcourt or half-court area, while the weaker player or players (B) play into the full-court (singles or doubles) area. Player A is positioned behind the baseline center (T) and player B is positioned behind the opposite baseline center (T). Player A starts the rally or point with drop-feed serves to player B. Player A's shots may only land within the service court area, while player B may hit his shots anywhere within the boundaries of the singles court. These rules make the game challenging for both players, and players can play an entire match this way.

Variation
Adding the alley to the stronger player's singles court widens the play area for the weaker player, giving him or her more area to hit in. At the same time, lessening the playing area for the stronger player makes him or her focus more on controlling shots within a smaller area. This approach creates an interesting match for the weaker player. A less-skilled player can request that the stronger player hit all balls past the service line in a baseline drill. This twist puts pressure on the stronger player to hit the ball deep in the backcourt, thus giving the weaker player an advantage. These are just a few examples of ways to even the playing field, but there are many more. Be creative and come up with variations that cater to the players' specific strengths and weaknesses.

Tip
Allowing weaker players to use the two-bounce rule helps to increase their on-court footwork, dexterity, and hand-eye coordination.

68—STROKE HANDICAP

Objective

This drill helps balance two players of different ability so players at different levels can compete against each other.

Description

Playing a weaker opponent's strongest shot can provide the advanced player with a challenging match. The weaker player has more confidence and consistency on his or her stronger side and thus can give the stronger player more balls to hit.

Execution

After deciding which side of the weaker player's game is stronger, forehand or backhand, the stronger player delivers all shots, including serves, to that side. Another method of handicapping is to not allow the stronger player to put the ball away against the weaker player. By requiring the stronger player to hit every ball back to the opponent, the weaker player can give the stronger player a challenging match. Players should try to play individual points, games, and then an entire match using this method.

Variation

To develop a weaker player's game further, both players can use a particular type of spin on all shots. For example, hitting a slice shot off both sides can even out an otherwise lopsided match. The stronger player or players may only win points by hitting a specific stroke to end the point. For example, the stronger player may only hit a volley, forehand, or backhand to end the point. The stronger player may be required to hit a certain number of balls in play before the point officially starts. For example, the stronger player may be required to hit five shots over the net before the actual point begins. Another way to stroke handicap a stronger player is by allowing the weaker opponent to win a point automatically if he or she is able to keep a certain number of balls in play against the stronger player. For example, if the weaker player keeps six balls in play before missing he or she automatically wins the point.

Tip

When competing against a weaker player, a stronger player can apply pressure by maintaining concentration and playing a little faster than the opponent, or vice versa if the weaker player has trouble keeping up.

69—SCORE HANDICAP

Objective

This drill equalizes different game styles by giving a score advantage to the weaker player. This method puts mental pressure on the stronger player, making him or her play tighter and harder to win the game, and it gives the weaker player the confidence to play well against the stronger player.

Description

A common way to handicap the game is to spot an opponent points in a game, such as 15-love or 30-love to start. This helps motivate the player who has fallen behind, usually the stronger of the two.

Execution

The weaker player or team receives a certain number of points before the first point of the game is played. Giving a combination of games and points can even out almost any match. For example, a player who is two to three levels less advanced than the opponent could receive four games and a 30-love lead in every game. An expansion of this method is to use negative numbers to handicap the stronger player by starting him or her with two fewer points or giving the weaker player two additional points in a game. The stronger player or players must fight back from a deficit. For example, the losing or lesser skilled player receives a 15-love or a 30-love lead only after starting to fall behind in the set. When a player falls behind or is losing, the player who is winning will spot the player who is losing one or two points per game until that player can catch up in the game, set, or match.

Variation

Play 11-point games and spot the weaker player 6 points to start with. The stronger player can also be required to achieve a certain number of points before the weaker player acquires a certain number of points. For example, players may play a 15-point game and if the weaker player acquires 3 points before the stronger player acquires 15 points, then the weaker player wins the match. Another possibility is if the weaker player wins two points in a row, then the stronger player must forfeit two points. If the weaker player wins three points in a row, then the stronger player forfeits three of his or her points. Players may set their own score handicap before the game or match begins. Try to think of other variations on the score handicap as well; these are just a few examples.

70—DOUBLE CUBE

Objective

Every time a player or team wins a game, the stakes for losing can double. This method will help motivate the losing player or team to play harder.

Description

The doubling cube or wager used in backgammon can put a cool twist into a set of tennis. The cube or wager should double the stakes every time the stronger team wins a game.

Execution

If player A breaks player B's serve while playing a set, player A may elect to double the stakes. (Two shuttle runs at the end of the set could be the wager, and the double would make it four shuttle runs). If player B continues the set, he or she may have an opportunity to redouble player A by making a comeback and getting into a position to win. If player B redoubles, the wager becomes eight shuttle runs, four times the original stakes. Pressure can sometimes equalize ability levels because when a bet is on the line most players play a bit more cautiously.

Variation

Players can play an eight-game pro set. If the weaker player wins three or four games before the stronger player wins eight, the weaker player wins the match.

71—TENNIS FOOTBALL

Objective

This drill develops footwork, dexterity, hand-eye coordination, fast reaction to the ball, and rapid change of direction.

Description

Football terminology gives an entertaining twist to this offense-defense drill. The drill requires players to win three consecutive points to score a game point. The game is over when a player or team scores 11 points.

Execution

Players A and B are positioned on opposite baselines. The football (tennis ball) starts at the 50-yard line (the tennis net), where a server feeds the ball. Each time a player wins a point, the player moves up 10 yards inside the opponent's area (to the service line). When the opponent wins a point, the football (tennis ball and players) moves back to the baseline. Field goals (clear winners) can be kicked (hit) only from 30 yards out or closer (inside the service boxes). Extra points after the touchdown (winning shot) also require another point to be played. If the extra point is won, the winning player or team collects the first game and the game continues. Players serve only if they continue to win points; otherwise, the opponent serves.

72—SMALL CHANGE

Objective
Making just one small change in a stronger player's game can equalize a match between players of different ability.

Description
Colossal changes aren't required to grow the game of tennis. Coaches or players can make small changes that will make tennis more fun and increase participation. Each of the drills handicaps a stronger player's game and helps a weaker player.

Execution
Eliminate the third set and play a tiebreaker instead. Eliminate side changes and change only at the end of the set. Eliminate let serves and first serves so that all shots will be played the same, including the serve. Eliminate the singles sticks so that net height will be the same for both singles and doubles. Play the best of four- or five-game sets. Like other sports, junior tennis must have special concessions for participants' age, skill, and ability level.

73—NET RUSHER EQUALIZATION

Objective
This drill gives players many options on how to handle an opponent who likes to rush up to the net and end the point early.

Description
How does a player return serve against the net rusher? The primary goal of the receiver is to return the serve low and at the net rusher's feet, forcing him or her to volley up so that the receiver can move in and crush it.

Execution
When an opponent takes control of the net, players can try passing down the line or lobbing over the opponent's head. They can pick on the opponent's weaker side up at the net or, if the opponent is a great wide volleyer, try to smack it right up the middle. Players should hit the ball off the rise so that they can close in faster than the opponent can and use tremendous topspin. Players can keep the opponent from moving in too close by attacking the ball in this manner. Above all, if players are unsuccessful in returning one way, they should change and try something different.

Tip
Remember to "tweak" your game plan to adjust to different styles of play. Don't completely abandon your plan; just adjust it until you find your groove.

74—MASTER BASELINER EQUALIZATION

Objective

These drilling tactics should be on the court with every player who has encountered the baseliner game style. The tactics will neutralize master baseliners' games and force them to play out of their comfort zone.

Description

Baseline masters lock themselves three to five feet behind the baseline and can hit and run until the cows come home. They are in top physical condition because they run down every shot thrown their way. Their strategy is to keep the ball coming back with high net clearance, to take few chances, and to wait until the opponent makes the first mistake. These drills help players develop ways to draw baseliners out of position and capitalize on their weaknesses, thus neutralizing their strengths.

Execution

Players should hit drop and angled shots any time the baseliner hits the ball short into the player's court. This tactic will force the master baseliner to move up to the net where the player can take advantage of the situation with a passing shot or lob. The serve-and-volley tactic is a great way to draw this anchor up off the baseline and force him or her to make different shot choices. Players should play a set using this method of counterattack. When players meet a master baseliner in a real match, they will be prepared.

Variation

Patience is the key to this drill. Players must learn to build the point one shot at a time. They should try different spins, sharper angles, drop shots, lobs, and approach the net whenever possible. Players must take the master baseliners out of their game by drawing them up to the net and then sending them scrambling back to recover a deeply hit lob. Any shot combination that incorporates the use of short shots, angles, lobs, and volleys will cause master baseliners to lose their focus and fall off balance.

Tip

Players must never fall into the trap of trying to outrally a master baseliner. Instead, they should mix up their shots to force the baseliner out of position, or else bring a sleeping bag, oxygen, and a night light. They could be out there a long time.

Lleyton Hewitt

Sneaky Tall or Competitive Beast?

© Human Kinetics

Age 22, height five-feet-10, weight 150 pounds, right-handed. Lleyton Hewitt has been called the ATP master counterpuncher. Standing just five-feet-10, he was nicknamed "Sneaky Tall" by the Davis Cup captain back in 1998 while playing in Adelaide, Australia, alongside his hero Patrick Rafter. The team captain believed that Hewitt wasn't built for quick finishes, which translated into Hewitt's becoming a human backboard. Hewitt is a master at keeping the ball in play and running his opponents into the ground. He attributes his success to his phenomenal footwork and love for the game. Hewitt began his tennis career at age 4. He played tennis 12 hours per day and by age 8 was winning matches against children much older than he was. Hewitt's first professional title was in 1998 in Adelaide, Australia. Although Hewitt became the number-one player on the ATP tour in 2002-03, was Player of the Year, and achieved his goal of winning the U.S. Open, he still feels that he needs to improve on certain areas of his game. But that's a well-kept secret, so it's back to drilling tactics and strategy.

75—POWER PLAYER EQUALIZATION

Objective
This drilling tactic gives players enlightenment on how to neutralize the power player's game.

Description
Power players usually have a favorite side so players should look for them to work the point to set up that weapon. This drilling tactic will help players identify opportunities to attack a power player's weakness and then take advantage of it.

Execution
Players should try to throw off the power player's game with different shots and different types of spin, including junk balls. Those tactics will drive a power player crazy. Patience is the name of the game. Players must try to slow the game to force power players to rush and make mistakes. Power players thrive off power. The harder their opponents hit, the harder they hit.

Tip
Players must avoid falling into the trap of playing the power game. The match will be over before they can ask, "What's the score?"

76—BASELINE COUNTERPUNCHER EQUALIZATION

Objective
This tactic helps players identify when the opponent is about to unleash a hidden weapon.

Description
When ready to strike, players position themselves just behind the baseline. They then step inside the baseline to catch the ball on the rise and smack a winner. They don't just sit back, push the ball, and let the opponent make the mistake. They take the initiative by building up the point to where they can attack.

Execution
When encountering a baseline counterpuncher, players should take some pace off the ball but keep the counterpuncher deep in the backcourt. Counterpunchers flourish off power, so players should hit behind them to offset their balance and rhythm. Players should mix up their shots and bring counterpunchers to the net to open up their weaknesses. Counterpunchers love to use the open stance coupled with heavy topspin and can usually place the ball with severe angles. They dislike stepping into the ball, so slice shots and drop shots can be effective. Above all, players must not let counterpunchers dictate the pace.

Tip
Players must mix up the pace and not try to overpower the counterpuncher.

77—PUSHER EQUALIZATION

Objective

These tactical methods help players make smart, aggressive shot selections when faced with this type of game style.

Description

Few defeats are more agonizing than one administered by a pusher. Sometimes called a human backboard, a pusher can keep the ball going all day long, usually with very little pace. These tactical solutions will help players learn how to build the point to hit aggressive winners, build the point to cut down on unforced errors, and create opportunities to open up the court and end the points early.

Execution

By forcing opponents to play extra balls, a pusher tempts players to overplay their shots (going for the line instead of a safe leeway inside or next to the line). Players should avoid this trap by playing smart and being patient. Unless a player is rated a 5.0 or above, trying to overpower a pusher is a poor idea. A smart tactic is to hit lots of volleys with angles and hit behind a pusher, thus wrong footing him or her. A pusher has a way of softening shots and slapping them back, so a good pattern to establish throughout a match is to create gaps on the court by taking advantage of angles. Moving a pusher out wide forces him or her out of the comfort zone, making them more likely to make errors and allowing players to take advantage of the pusher's weaknesses.

Tip

Playing against the pusher can cause players to choke. They may be overwhelmed by thoughts like, "Oh no, what will people think of me if I lose to this player?" Here a few player-tested strategies to incorporate into your game plan. Players must approach the pusher with respect, but not be overwhelmed by the pusher's strategy. Players should play their game and play aggressive at the appropriate time during the point, remembering to play the ball, not their opponent. Once the match starts, they must close their mind to all outside or inside distractions and stay centered in the moment. They should play point for point, not one point in the past or one point in the future, and stick with their game plan, tweaking only when necessary. Finally, players must be careful when hitting a ball behind a slow opponent, because the opponent may still be there. Players instead should try hitting more to the open court area that they have created.

78—HACKER EQUALIZATION

Objective

These tactical methods help players think and play the ball instead of the opponent, make smart shot choices, and become better at ball placement.

Description

Patience is the name of the game when playing hackers. If they are allowed to rule the match, their unorthodox mechanics will drive opponents batty. Players should avoid playing the hacker's game by pushing the ball back to him or her—it's like feeding spinach to Popeye.

Execution

The winning bet in dealing with hackers is to move them all over the court by using every stroke known to tennis. This maneuver forces the hacker's game plan to fall apart. Because of the hacker's unstable hitting positions, weird grips, and wacky uncontrolled spins, players must be ready to move quickly for balls that are spinning in all sorts of weird ways. Players should be aggressive but avoid going for winner after winner. Building up the point and creating opportunities is an effective approach. Players should be patient, wait for the right ball, and then attack.

Tip

Players must avoid being caught up in watching the hacker's unorthodox ways of executing strokes or shots. Watching the show will pull players into the hacker's trap.

chapter 9

Strategic Game Planning

Executing and consistently practicing strategic drills for singles and doubles will help players acquire the skill and speed necessary to play effectively and enjoyably. In the words of Mr. Bill Tilden, "Singles is a game of speed, doubles a game of finesse." Success is largely due to confidence, and players have confidence when they know and stick to what they do best. Through specific and repetitious practice, players can build their strengths and improve their weaknesses. The stronger their game, the more likely they are to succeed with a strategic game plan in a match.

Drilling with a purpose in mind helps players improve, correct weaknesses, learn new skills, and understand how to incorporate them into a strategic game plan for competition. Drills are routines that allow players to hit a large number of balls in short periods, thus helping them use their court time efficiently and effectively. Drilling reinforces proper stroke production, allows players to groove their shots, improves overall court movement and physical conditioning, and allows players to practice situations that occur frequently during match play. A drill may be entertaining, exciting, and complicated, but if it doesn't closely simulate the shots or situations that occur in a match, it is a waste of time. Drills should be simple, specific, entertaining, exciting, and educational. Most important, they must simulate situations of actual match play.

The following chapter is filled with effective drills that can sharpen playing skills. Drilling will help players prepare for the pressure of singles and doubles during tournament or practice match-play competition.

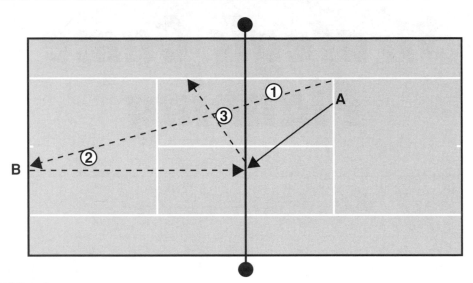

Objective

This drill teaches court and ball control.

Description

The drill puts players in the perfect position to pass the net person and shows the consequences for a failed attempt.

Execution

Player A stands behind the service line, and player B stands on the opposite baseline. Using only half the court and the alley, player A starts the point by hitting the ball deep to player B. Player A closes in to the net. Player B may not lob on the first return, but after that, anything goes. If player A wins the point, he or she starts the next point from the same position at the service line. If player A loses, he or she slides back to the baseline and player B slides up to the service line and starts the next point. They play to 15 or 21.

Variation

Players can try this drill crosscourt including the alley. In addition, both players can start on the baseline using only half the court (doubles alley is included). Player A starts the point by drop hitting a deep ground stroke. Play continues until one player hits short. The player who has to return the short shot must then come into the net and continue to play the point to completion. Play continues to 15 or 21, with serve exchange every five serves.

Tip

If players find that too many of their shots are landing short, they should check to see that they are completely following through to the target. If they tend to hit with excessive topspin, they may be pulling off the ball early, which will also cause shots to fall short.

80—CROSSCOURT AND DOWN THE LINE

Objective

This drill practices depth control, footwork, consistency, ball direction, and on-court conditioning.

Description

Isolating any stroke helps solidify it. This drill forces players to use good footwork, the ready hop, quick recovery skills, and racket-head control to hit to a designated area of the court.

Execution

Players position themselves on the baseline. Player A hits forehands crosscourt to player B's forehand. Both players hit toward the deuce-court area and use doubles alleys to create sharper angles and more hitting room. While players A and B are hitting crosscourt, two additional players can hit crosscourt toward the advantage-court area. One or two balls can be in play at the same time. Players rally crosscourt or down the line and work on consistently keeping the ball deep past the service line.

Variations

Players can try having only one ball in play. Two players hit only down the line, and the other two hit only crosscourt. Or one player can return every ball crosscourt, while the opponent returns every shot down the line. The first to 11 points wins. Another variation is to have one player put the ball in play with a ground stroke. Players then attempt a continuous down-the-line or crosscourt rally while using all stances, spins, power adjustments, and angle placement. Targets may be placed on the court for better concentration and target control. Players play to 11 points.

Tip

Precision footwork and conditioning gained through drilling crosscourt and down the line ground strokes or volleys will help players of all levels physically and mentally outlast many long, grueling, closely-contested matches. Players must learn that there is more to tennis footwork than just running after the ball. Great footwork combines the gracefulness of a ballet dancer, the reflexes of a boxer, and the timing of a basketball player. This drill will also get players into top tennis shape. If they can do this drill using all the variations for one hour and then walk without wobbling, they are tennis machines!

81—CRAZY 8 VOLLEY

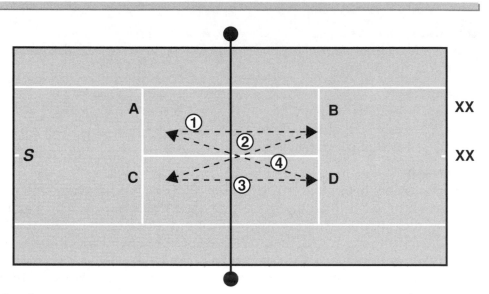

Objective
This fast-paced drill challenges players' ability to volley under stress and develops quick hands and feet.

Description
Using a set pattern, players try to keep the ball going without missing.

Execution
Player A starts the action by hitting to player B, positioned directly in front of player A. Player B volleys diagonally across the net to player C. Player C volleys straight ahead across the net to player D, and player D volleys diagonally across the net back to player A. Players do not allow the ball to bounce. Scoring is optional.

Variation
All players are positioned up at the net across from each other. Players A and B, who are partners, volley all balls down the line. Players C and D, who are partners, volley all balls crosscourt. All play is up at the net. Scoring is optional. Play is with two players for singles or four players for doubles.

Tip
Players who are afraid of the net should first practice volleying against a backboard to develop the confidence and reflexes it takes to beat the net jitters and hit effective, aggressive volleys. Remember, quick hands combined with quick feet make any player, no matter the level, hard to beat!

82—THREE-HIT CYCLE

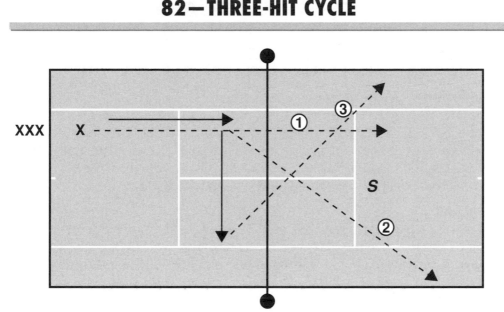

Objective

This drill develops the combination of steps that players need to become proficient at the net. It develops good split stepping, the approach shot, and the feeling of skills for closing in on the net.

Description

This sweet combination of shots helps players develop footwork skills, confidence, finesse, and anticipation skills.

Execution

The server, positioned inside one of the service boxes, feeds three shots in from the opposite side of the net. All players should be standing three to four feet behind the service line, behind either the deuce or advantage service-court area. The first player in line hits a forehand approach shot down the line, closes in for a backhand volley crosscourt, and finishes with an attack forehand volley crosscourt. The player returns to the end of the line. The second player moves in for a backhand approach shot down the line, closes in for a forehand volley crosscourt, and finishes with an attack backhand volley crosscourt. Players should keep the three-hit cycle drill moving so that they don't become listless and lazy waiting in line.

Tip

Players should use the ready hop before hitting the approach and the split step before hitting the volley.

83—TEN-BALL SINGLES

Objective

This drill helps develop stamina, consistency, and footwork.

Description

By having to play hard-to-reach balls in different areas of the singles court, players get a sense of court coverage and build confidence in their ability to run down any shot that may come their way. This type of drilling also helps players develop the graceful footwork needed to be able to move side to side and up and back at any given moment during match play.

Execution

Players take a position behind the baseline in single file. One player steps up to center (T) on the baseline. A server feeds balls anywhere on the singles court, feeding forehands, backhands, drop shots, and lobs. The player must hit 10 consecutive shots in play. For every shot the player misses, the server deducts 1 point. For example, if the player hits 5 consecutive shots and misses shot number 6, he or she drops to number 5. The goal is to reach 10 consecutive shots without missing. Later, the goal can increase to 15 or 20.

Variation

One player starts behind the baseline, and two or three other players play the net. A server starts each point by feeding the ball to different places on the court, and the baseline player tries to win the point. The volleyers try to stop the player from accomplishing this. Players can move anywhere to retrieve the shots hit by the singles player, but they must return to their position up at the net after the point ends. Play continues until the player wins 20 points. Players rotate so that each takes a position up at the net. Players can also try a 50-point drill. The player receives 2 points for every outright passing shot but only 1 point for a point won by having to play out the point.

Tip

If at any time during match play you are required to retreat back to the baseline to recover a deeply placed lob, start moving for the ball before the ball reaches the net tape. If you take a moment to process the action, it's too late. Forget it and congratulate your opponent for a well-placed shot.

84—UP AND BACK

Objective
This drill develops backcourt players' experience in hitting deep defensive lobs and teaches them how to play aggressively when returning a partner's overhead.

Description
This drill helps players make smart recovery choices and stay balanced when having to move up to the net and then quickly back to recover the overhead and place it effectively.

Execution
Both players take positions on the baseline at opposite ends of the court. Player A alternately hits drives and lobs to player B. When returning the hit, player B alternates between volleys and overheads. Player B must move up to the net for the volley and back for the overhead. Scoring is optional.

Variation
Player A positions behind the baseline on one side of the court, either deuce or advantage court, and player B is up at the net diagonally from player A. Player A uses a combination of drives and lobs when hitting shots, and player B uses a combination of volleys and overheads. The first player to win 15 or 21 points is the winner.

85—FIVE-BALL OVERHEAD SEQUENCE

Objective
This drill helps players learn how to set up to hit an effective overhead and how to recover in balanced position and be ready to hit another.

Description
Many players allow the ball to drift behind their heads when attempting to hit overheads. This drill helps players learn to hit overheads when the ball is behind them and to close in on the net after hitting the overhead.

Execution
Player A takes a position up at the net. Player B is on the baseline opposite player A. Player B starts the sequence of shots to player A. Player B feeds a deep lob to player A. Player A hits an aggressive overhead, closes in, and taps the net. The instant player A taps the net, player B throws up another lob to player A. The sequence continues until player A hits five successful overheads.

86—SIX-BALL PATTERN SEQUENCE

Objective

This drill develops concentration and consistency and identifies weaknesses in a player's game.

Description

By having to respond to a mix of shots, players learn how to play all shots, get a feel for the next shot, and sharpen starts, stops, and the split step.

Execution

Player A takes a position behind the baseline, and player B is up at the net. Player A feeds six balls to player B in the following sequence: a forehand volley, a backhand volley, a deep lob over player B's head, a short ball to the forehand for an approach down the line, one backhand volley, and finally a lob for an overhead smash. The pattern may be altered.

87—CRISS-CROSS VOLLEY POACH

Objective

This drill develops poaching and volleying skills.

Description

Poaching is intercepting the receiver's return of serve. When attempting to poach, players must communicate with their partners and be proficient at volleying.

Execution

Players form two single-file lines behind the service boxes next to the center (T). A server feeds a volley to the first player in one of the lines. That player volleys down the line or crosscourt, immediately crosses over for a backhand poach, and hits it crosscourt. After completing the poached volley, the player moves to the end of the opposite line. Players should move diagonally forward for the poach shot.

Variation

Players divide into two lines behind the baseline close to the center (T). A server feeds wide forehands to one side and wide backhands to the other (simultaneously). Immediately after hitting, players crisscross to the end of the opposite line. The server keeps players moving by hitting to one side and then the other.

Tip

The net person can bluff by pretending to intercept the return of serve but then return to the usual position. The bluff can elicit a down-the-line shot right back at the bluffer, who can make an easy volley.

88—APPROACH SHOT, VOLLEY, OVERHEAD

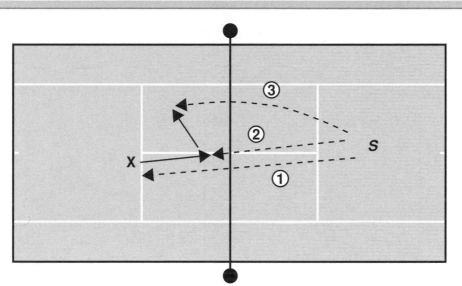

Objective
This drill helps the intermediate player (3.0 to 3.5) develop quick thinking and quick reflexes during match-play simulation.

Description
This drill slows the action a bit. By isolating specific strokes and combining them into a pattern, players learn when and where to hit offensive shots during singles or doubles match-play competition.

Execution
Players take positions behind the service line. A server hits a ball to the first player in line, who must return it with a forehand or backhand approach shot down the line. Immediately, the player moves to the net to prepare for another ball from the server and must return it using a forehand or backhand volley. For the next hit, the server throws up a lob, and the player must shift diagonally and backward across the center service line and return the ball using an overhead. The player moves to the end of the line, and the next player waiting moves up to play.

Variation
A server feeds balls to the players who are positioned on the baseline. The baseline players try to drive the ball past the opponents up at net on the opposite side of the net. Players can use any combination of shots to play out and win points. They play 11 points and then rotate clockwise one position at a time.

Tip
Players should use the approach shot when the court surface is fast to put pressure on the opponent, who will have less time to prepare to return the shot. Also, a wind at the player's back will add speed to the shot and cause the opponent to rush his or her shots.

89—CHIP APPROACH AND TOUCH VOLLEY

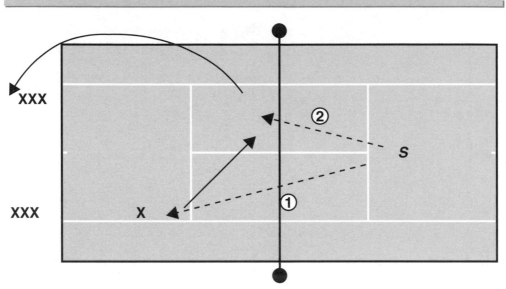

Objective

This drill introduces the beginning stages of finesse skills and in time creates the rhythmic footwork needed for those kinds of shots.

Description

Touch or finesse shots in tennis require players to develop a sense of being able to feel the ball on the racket. Developing good touch or feel adds a new dimension to any player's game. This technique affords players more place-ment strategy than just plain smacking the ball 100 percent of the time. Place-ment more than power wins points, not the other way around.

Execution

Players form two lines—one line behind the deuce court and the other behind the advantage court. The first player in the deuce line hits an approach shot fed in by a server down the singles sideline. The player then moves diagonally forward to approach the net and hit a superwide volley, attempting to hit a crosscourt touch volley. The player then proceeds to the end of the advantage-court line. One side hits a forehand approach and a backhand touch volley crosscourt, and the other side hits a backhand approach with a forehand touch volley. Players can start the drill slowly and gradually increase the pace of the rotation to work on developing a quick split step and closing in diagonally to the net to hit the volley.

Tip

Developing a touch game makes any player a smarter and more dangerous competitor to reckon with.

90—OSCILLATION VOLLEY

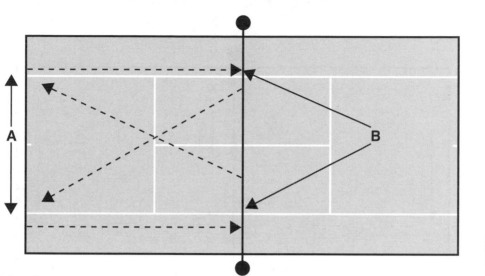

Objective

This drill develops quick rhythmic footwork, fast reaction to the ball, change of direction with recovery, volley placement, and sound ground stroking.

Description

Running wide for alternating forehands and backhands is called oscillation. This drill helps players improve ground-stroking skills, footwork, and consistency.

Execution

Player A takes a position behind the baseline, and player B plays the net. Player A hits ground strokes down the line only, and player B, the volleyer, hits crosscourt only. Both players move with the ball or shot. Player A hits a forehand down the line to player B's backhand volley, if player B is right-handed. Player B volleys crosscourt to player A's backhand. Player A returns a backhand shot down the line to players B's forehand volley. Player B volleys this shot crosscourt again. They keep this pattern going as long as they can. Because this is a consistency drill, there is no scoring. Rotation is optional.

Variations

Player A is behind the baseline, and player B is up at the net. Both players use only one side of the court and return to the center (T) each time after hitting. The volleyer hits forehand volleys to the baseline player's backhand. They rotate positions. Another variation is for the player or players in line behind the baseline to start at the center (T). A server positioned at the net on the other side feeds alternating shots to the player's forehand and backhand.

Tip

The racket face controls the direction of shots. The ball goes in the direction the strings are facing because it bounces off the racket at right angles.

91—HIT THE VOLLEYER AND RUN

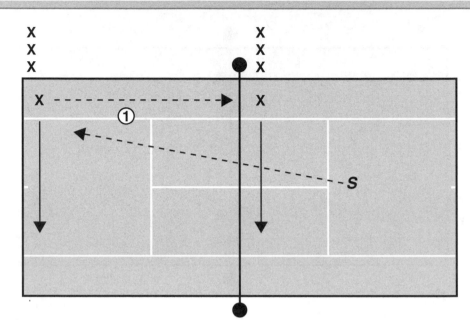

Objective

This drill helps players learn how to pass on the run, recover quickly, and build total court coverage, confidence, agility, and speed.

Description

Running to hit any shot in tennis takes tremendous footwork, good timing, and good shot selection. The player must recover and set up for the return. This drill helps players isolate and practice running down ground strokes, recovering, and deciding where to hit.

Execution

Two or three players start behind the baseline on one side of the court. Two or three other players position themselves up at the net on the opposite side but on the same side as the baseliners so that they are facing each other. A server feeds a ground stroke to the first baseliner in line, who hits the shot down the line to the volleyer. They move across the court together. The server feeds another ball to the baseliner, who hits another down-the-line shot to the same volleyer on the opposite side of the court. They proceed to the end of their respective lines, and the next two players move into position. They repeat this drill starting on the opposite side of the court.

Tip

When players are at the net and a ball is coming straight at them at high speed, they should shift their thoughts to backhand safety. The backhand covers more area than the forehand or "ducking" will.

Objective

This drill helps players develop quick bursts of speed and intersperse them with the step slide to allow recovery into proper position to hit the next shot. Stroking the incoming ball effectively requires the body, legs, and feet to be in the best position possible.

Description

The ability to recover effectively after running down a shot determines whether a player will be able to stay in the point or lose the point. If a player is still trying to regain balance after hitting the first shot, he or she will probably lose the point.

Execution

Player A takes a position up at the net, and player B is positioned at the intersection of the opposite baseline and sideline. Player B must make a recovery to this area after each ground stroke. Player B may hit shots down the line, crosscourt, or a combination of shots. Player A hits the first ball to player B, the second to the center of the court, and the third to the far sideline. They keep this drill going until player B hits a set of shots without missing. They then switch positions. Players can rotate after each sequence of shots.

Tip

Balance is crucial in tennis. By incorporating the step slide into their recovery, players can move in any direction.

93—QUICK VOLLEY

Objective
This drill develops quick reflexes, footwork, and hand-eye-ball control.

Description
Players can perform this practice tool before match play as a warm-up drill. The drill helps players improve footwork, quicken reflexes, and gain better ball and court sense.

Execution
One or two players take positions at the net and volley straight ahead to each other or diagonally across to each other. If two players are drilling, both players are up at the net facing each other. If four players are drilling, two are on each side, facing each other. Players hit the ball using a forehand or backhand volley, keeping the ball in play without allowing it to bounce. As players improve, the speed of the balls can increase and players can alternate between forehand and backhand volley exchanges. Players should split step with every stroke of the ball, and after each hit they should split step before striking the ball.

Variation
Players A and B stand on opposite service lines. They volley back and forth, moving in with each shot to within one foot of the net. Once players have mastered closing in, they can back up with each volley and then close back in.

94—SINGLE-FILE VOLLEY APPROACH

Objective
This drill slows the pace so that players can learn how to approach the net and set up to hit a volley.

Description
This drill allows players to focus on developing smart midcourt play.

Execution
A server takes a position on the service line, and players line up behind the opposite service line. One at a time, players close in to the net, split step, and then hit a forehand or backhand volley. After volleying, the player backpedals to the end of the line, and the next player moves forward. The server can increase the number of volleys or mix up forehand and backhand volleys.

Variation
Players line up at the net post, and a server hits balls from the opposite side. The first player in line sidesteps to the center of the court, taps the center net tape, turns sideways to sidestep backward, and then returns a ball by hitting an overhead. The player then closes to the net to return another ball using a volley.

95—SHORT BALL

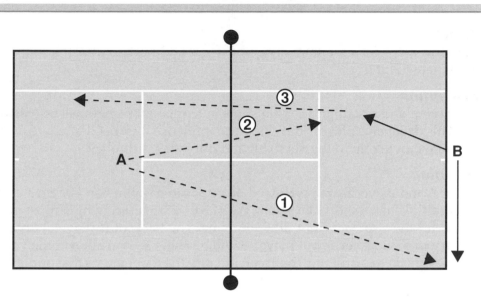

Objective

This drill develops good reaction time and a feel for identifying and hitting short balls.

Description

This drill helps players to identify the short ball, have the confidence to move in and attack it, hit it to a designated area, and follow it up to the net to finish the point.

Execution

Player A takes a position at the service line and hits deep balls to player B, who is positioned at the opposite baseline. Player B hits the deep ball back to a designated area on the court, which can be anywhere predetermined by the players. Player A then hits a short shot to player B, who attempts to retrieve the shot and place it aggressively away from player A. Player A should try to hit to a specified area of the court.

Variation

A server stands at the net post just off the court and feeds a short ball to one of the backcourt players, A or B, who are positioned on the baseline standing opposite each other. The receiving player hits an approach shot and closes in on the net. The opponent tries to pass or lob to win the point. They play 11-point games and then rotate positions.

96—CROSSCOURT RALLY ATTACK

Objective

This drill helps increase knowledge of when and how to attack a short ball and where to hit it.

Description

Identifying and reacting to certain shots in tennis can sometimes be frustrating. This drill helps players develop the confidence they need to move in and continue moving up to the net to hit and put away the volley.

Execution

Player A and player B are positioned on opposite baselines and begin a crosscourt rally. When a short ball arises, the player who is receiving it must move in and hit the approach shot down the line. The backcourt player, player A, may try to pass player B, but player B will be ready to hop all over the volley. The players do this drill until both can identify the movements that opponents make just before they try to unleash a devastating passing shot.

Tip

Anticipation is a learned response. The more players play, the more they learn to "feel" the kind of return the opponent may hit. Anticipation of the short ball definitely makes hitting the approach shots easier.

97—RISING STAR

Objective

This drill helps players develop quick bursts of speed and intersperse them with the step slide to recover to the proper position to hit the next shot. Stroking the incoming ball effectively requires the body, legs, and feet to be in the best position possible.

Description

This drill helps players learn to hit to a specific area, recover, get back into position, prepare to hit again to a specific area, recover, and get back into position again. The drill builds strong recovery skills.

Execution

Player A is on the right side of the baseline, and player B is at the center of the opposite baseline. Player A begins by hitting alternating crosscourt and down-the-line shots to player B. Player B must hit every ball back to player A. After several minutes they rotate sides.

98—SHORT COURT

Objective

This drill helps players learn to control the pace of the ball in a restricted area of the court while developing the building blocks they need to execute finesse shots.

Description

This drill isolates finesse shots by permitting players to use only touch shots and touch volleys.

Execution

Two or more players can perform this drill. They must keep within the service-court area, one on either side of the net. Players attempt to use touch and angle shots to keep the ball in play. They must hit 10 to 15 consecutive shots before using the shot in a game.

99—DEEP SHOT

Objective

This drill helps players learn how to hit deep penetrating ground strokes from the baseline with confidence.

Description

The drill forces players to keep the ball deep in the court or suffer the unforced error of hitting too short. Players need to learn how to place the ball deep in the backcourt area consistently and with aggressive confidence.

Execution

Positioned on the baseline, player A starts the rally with a deeply fed ball to player B, who is positioned at the opposite baseline. Play continues until a ball lands on or inside the service-court area. The player who hits short loses the point. Two or four players can perform this drill. They play 11-point games.

Variation

Players can use the service boxes or full half court including the doubles alley. They can try going crosscourt short court first and then slowly slide back to the baseline. They can try playing an entire match within the service-court area, or they can try to keep the ball in play using only half of the court within the service-court area.

100 — HALF-COURT HUSTLE

Objective
This drill works on improving footwork, agility, and speed during match-play simulation.

Description
This drill forces players to change direction and sprint short distances many times in the span of one minute. Tennis is all about short bursts of speed, and players need dexterity to react and recover with balance and confidence.

Execution
Player A positions up at the net, and player B stands on the service line. Player A hits soft-angled volleys that force player B to run. Player B must tap each ball back to player A. If a ball is missed, player A immediately puts the next one in play. Player B shouldn't stop hustling until one minute has elapsed.

Tip
Players must keep their feet moving at all times while on court. If they stop moving, they're dead in the water.

101 — APPROACH SHOT, PASSING SHOT

Objective
This drill aids in the development of strong passing shots while simulating match play.

Description
Approach shots are ground strokes played with the intention of following them up to the net to gain control of the net and attempt to hit a winning volley. This drill helps players gain the fundamental knowledge of when to hit an approach shot and where to hit it.

Execution
Players A, B, and C are positioned behind one baseline, and player D is positioned behind the opposite baseline. Players A, B, and C take turns hitting down-the-line approach shots to player D, who attempts to pass the approaching player. Players should play out the point. After one player accumulates 11 points, players rotate. No lobbing is allowed.

102—NET APPROACH

Objective
This drill develops clear and concise check-pause, split-step, or stutter-step techniques as well as good team communication skills.

Description
This drill teaches players how to communicate and move in effectively to hit an approach shot as a team.

Execution
Two players begin just in front of the baseline. With each shot fed in by a server, both move forward a few steps after one of them hits the shot. By the third or fourth shot, both players should be up at the net engaged in a rapid volley exchange. They keep executing the drill and increasing the pace of play. Players try to get up to the net as fast as possible.

Tip
Players should be certain to use a split step, landing on the balls of the feet with each volley.

103—ATTACK AND SMACK

Objective
This drill develops the serve-and-volley technique.

Description
Serving and volleying is an aggressive game plan for doubles match play. The team that incorporates this method in its doubles strategy will be a force to be reckoned with.

Execution
The server must serve and volley on every serve, first and second, or the team loses the point. They play a set using this method.

Tip
If the ball hits the net and drops onto the opponents' side of the court, the players should rush the net to cut off possible angles and force a low percentage shot that the opponents aren't capable of making.

104—HOT-PEPPER DOUBLES

Objective

This drill helps develop communication skills, teamwork, and the quick reflexes needed for outstanding net play.

Description

To develop quick reflexes for volleying and anticipating shot direction, this drill forces both players to stay in the frying pan without the option of backing out. Players work to build the confidence it takes to set up, attack, and win the point.

Execution

This drill is identical to the singles hot-pepper drill except that it involves four people and allows sharp-angled volleys. Players A and B play against players C and D. Teams are positioned behind the service line, each behind a service box facing each other. Player A starts the volley exchange by feeding the first ball, underhanded, to one of the players on the opposite side of the net. The fast-paced exchange continues until a player makes an error, hits a winning volley, or successfully hits a lob volley over an opponent. Players may hit around or through the middle of the opponents if they can find an opening. They play to 15 or 21 points and then rotate positions.

105—DOUBLES HUSTLE

Objective

This drill helps players learn how to move to different shots and areas of the court effectively with a partner while playing doubles.

Description

This exercise slows the pace of competitive play so that players learn when to take a shot, when to relinquish to the partner, and how to move together like well-oiled machinery.

Execution

The server positions up at the net with a large basket of balls. Team players A and B are positioned up at the net on the opposite side. The server gently feeds balls from side to side and down the middle of players A and B. When the ball is hit to the right, players A and B must move together to the right to hit the shot, trying to keep the same distance apart. Likewise, if the ball is hit to the left, both players should move together to try to hit the shot. If the ball goes up the middle, one player calls for it. Players must hit gently; this is not a drill for point playing. Whether the server lobs, drops, or whatever, both players must move together. They play consistently for two minutes straight.

106—DOUBLES APPROACH LOB AND RECOVERY

Objective

One key ingredient in doubles is learning to identify when to approach the net and how to recover after the opponent throws a lob over the team's heads.

Description

This drill helps a team learn how to take advantage of the short ball in doubles play, and in the event that one player is drawn back to the baseline, to return quickly to the offensive position.

Execution

Players A and B are positioned in standard doubles formation. The server or instructor is positioned on the opposite service line. The server feeds a short ball to player A, who hits an approach shot crosscourt and advances to the net with player B. The server returns the ball with a lob over player B's head. Player A recovers the ball and lobs it crosscourt. At the same time, player B moves over to cover the spot that player A vacated. Player A follows the high lob into the net again. The server returns the lob with a floater down the middle, which player B cuts off with an aggressive swinging volley. Play is continuous.

Variation

Have both players A and B start back on the baseline together. The server or instructor feeds a short ball to either player A or B. Both players should close in on the net. If player B hits the approach shot crosscourt, then the server would hit the lob over player B's head and player A would cross over and cover player B's vacated spot. Player B should return the lob with a crosscourt, deeply placed lob and work back down to the net. Play is continuous.

Tip

On the backhand approach shot or volley, it is vitally important that players remember to keep their shoulders sideways throughout the stroke. Players should use the semiwestern or full western grip so that they can put tremendous topspin on the swinging volley.

107—VOLLEY-LOB-VOLLEY

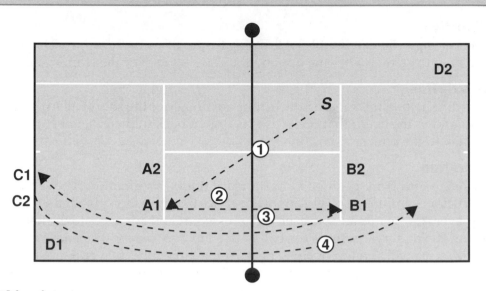

Objective

This drill helps players develop the disguised lob-volley shot and learn when and where to hit it during a simulated singles or doubles match.

Description

The lob volley, a rewarding and spectacular shot, has been described as a reverse overhead smash. It's a sneaky shot that players must practice in game situations. The stroke itself is a low volley that is suddenly lobbed with either topspin or slice, usually from inside the service-court area.

Execution

Players A1 and B1, who are positioned on the service line, move out wide toward the single sideline. The server feeds to player A1, who volleys the ball to player B1. Player B1, positioned opposite player A1, lob volleys the ball over player A1 to player C1, positioned on the baseline at the center (T). Player C1 finishes the sequence with a lob over player B1's head to the baseline. To spice things up a bit, four additional players can join and make this a doubles drill. Players A1 and A2 are positioned on the service line. Players B1 and B2 are positioned on the opposite service line, facing players A1 and A2. Players C1 and C2 are positioned on the baseline behind players A1 and A2. Two additional players wait to replace any player who flubs a shot. Player D1 waits off the court next to the baseline on the side of players C1 and C2. Player D2 waits off the court behind the opposite baseline. Players play 21-point games using this drilling method to start the points. Play doesn't start until the sequence of shots is successfully completed. After player C1 or players C1 and C2 hit the lob over player B1 or players B1 and B2, players are permitted to play out the point.

108—QUICK VOLLEY DROP OUT

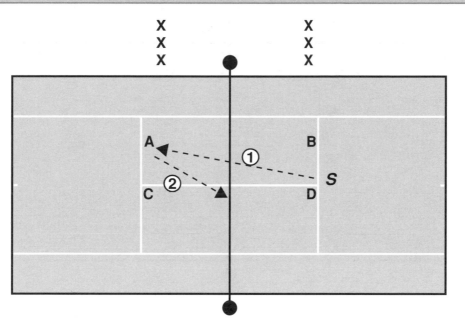

Objective
This drill helps develop quick hands and feet, stamina, ball sense, and control.

Description
By restricting play to the service-court area and not allowing the ball to drop, players develop the split-step method needed for sound volleying, quick hands, shot anticipation, and the confidence to stay in the mix when things heat up during competition.

Execution
Players A and C are positioned up at the net standing opposite players B and D. Any additional players wait off court ready to jump in when any player flubs a shot. To get the action started, the server feeds a ball to player A. Player A hits to either player B or player D. Play continues until a player lets the ball hit the ground. The point ends when a player lets the ball drop or misses outright. The next player in line takes a place. This is an individual exercise; players A and B are not partners, nor are players C and D.

Variation
Play can be with teams. Players can use the nondominant hand to build strength and control on both sides of the body.

Tip
When hitting crisp, penetrating volleys, players should not take the racket head back past the shoulder. Volleying against a backboard is a perfect way to develop the punching or blocking motion needed to hit volleys.

109—DOUBLES APPROACH-SHOT CHALLENGE

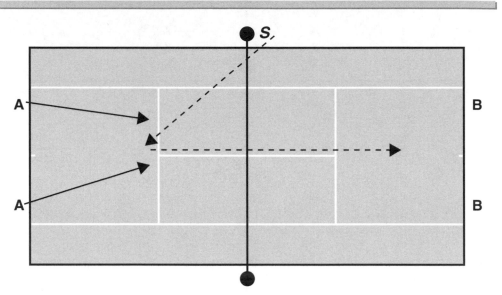

Objective

This drill helps develop the doubles low-ball and short-ball attack and defense, the approach shot, and the strategies of attacking the net by closing in or staying back to work the point.

Description

This drill isolates the approach shot and helps players learn to complete the approach to the net after hitting the approach shot.

Execution

Two teams position themselves behind opposite baselines. The server feeds team A a soft, short shot at the service line. The server should give each team two chances to put the ball in play. Team A must execute an approach shot and then close in to the net. The first team to win 21 points wins the match.

Variations

An extension of the first approach-shot challenge, this drill helps players identify the best shots to use for attacking and moving up to the net. Teams A and B are behind opposite baselines. To start, a server feeds a ball to team A. Both teams start rallying. When one team hits the ball into the service-court area of the opposite side of the court, the team receiving the short shot must approach the net together or automatically lose the point. Teams play out the point. The first team to win 21 points wins the match. Another variation is to have two teams a few feet behind the service line opposite each other. A server feeds a soft, low ball to team A, which will try to return it softly and low to team B. Both teams then close in toward the net and try to keep the ball low to close in behind and hit a winner.

110—ATTACK AND DEFEND DOUBLES CHALLENGE

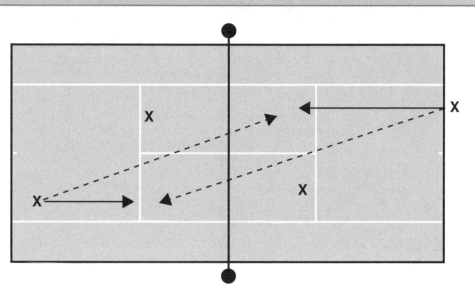

Objective

This drill helps reinforce the fundamentals of approaching the net, attacking and defending the net, and countering the attack up at the net.

Description

This drill works to set up play so that a preplanned shot forces a team to move up, hit an approach shot, and then commit to attacking the net. The drill also helps players learn how to defend against the net attack.

Execution

Four players take position in standard doubles formation. The server hits a second serve and follows it to the net. The receiver returns and moves up to the net. Players try to use soft, low volleys to force the opponent to volley up to them so that they can move in and hit a winner. If the receiver can hit the return early from well within the playing court and keep the return wide out into the alley, he or she has an excellent chance at winning the point up at the net. A well-placed return helps set up the point for solid volley winners. Players play out all points to completion.

Variation

The server is allowed to serve and volley crosscourt only. The receiver defends by staying back after the return and works the point by mixing high, deep lobs and drives.

Tip

After hitting a high, deep, penetrating lob, players should not sit back and watch the action but attack the net.

111—ROTATING APPROACH DOUBLES

Objective

This drill emphasizes closing in and attacking the net.

Description

This enjoyable drill helps players have fun hitting approach shots and volleys. The drill takes the pressure off having to decide who takes what shot and what the player does with it. This drill specifies who hits the approach shot, where the player hits it, and what happens after the player hits it.

Execution

Team A and team B start in standard doubles formation. Team A has been dubbed kings or queens of the hill. A server feeds an approach shot to one player of team A. The player hits the approach, and both players of team A move up to the net and play the point out against the opposing team. The challenging team, team B, must win 3 points in a row to knock the top team, team A, off the hill. If team B loses one of the points in the succession of points, then another waiting team rotates in. Team B must start from zero points again. The team that accumulates 21 points wins.

Variation

Players can use all three doubles formations—monster, standard, and Australian doubles.

Tip

Players should always hit their approach shots and volleys with slice or backspin. This tactic helps keep the ball low and forces the opponents to hit up on the ball, allowing players to move in and attack.

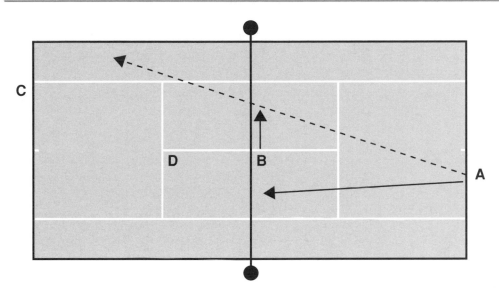

Objective

This drill develops poaching, serving, and volleying skills.

Description

The idea of using different formations in doubles is to take advantage of a weakness in the opposition, to block their strengths, to cover up a team's own weaknesses, or to use the team's strengths to their fullest. In the Australian formation, the server's partner stands in the same court as the server instead of standing in the opposite service court.

Execution

Players can play this aggressive form of doubles in three ways: The server's partner crosses on a sortie; the server's partner makes a sortie if possible, but the server crosses; or the server takes whichever side his or her partner doesn't take. *Sortie* is a French term that means to "strike out" or "exit" or "going out." In tennis, *sortie* means "to poach." Whichever method they decide to use, players should play it aggressively.

In the first style, the most popular one, the server, who is positioned behind the baseline, serves the ball either into the opponent's body or down the center (T). The server moves straight up to the net, while the partner poaches or crosses to the other side. This style gives the server the shortest route to the net, and the poacher distracts the receiver. Now both players are up at the net looking to end the point with a volley or overhead. They continue to use this formation until the server's game ends.

113—MONSTER DOUBLES

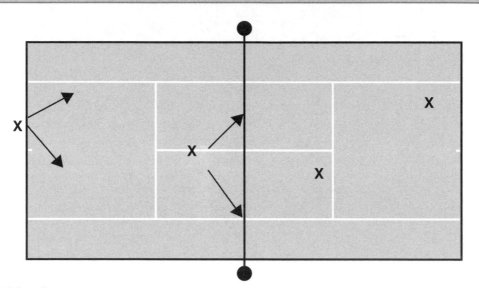

Objective

This drill helps a team keep the opposition off balance and improves serving, volleying, and poaching skills.

Description

This style of doubles play is a variation of the Australian doubles formation. The difference is the positioning of the serving team's net player. The net player of the serving team straddles the center service line up at the net. Now the net player of the serving team is in the perfect position for poaching directional signaling. Because the net player is positioned in the middle of the court up at the net, he or she must create directional signals to alert the partner about which direction he or she will attempt to poach. If the player poaches to the right, the server should cover the net or court to the net player's left. Players can invent their own method of signaling. This formation throws off the concentration of the opposing team. And it's fun!

Execution

The server's partner straddles the centerline, squatting and positioned approximately three feet from the net. Good communication is essential for this poaching style of play. The net player must poach to one side or the other at the sound of the partner's serve. By signaling the partner beforehand, the net player lets the server know which side to switch to after serving. By anticipating the direction of the service return, the net player can intercept or sortie the shot and volley it through the hole or at the opposing players' feet. Players play to 20 points or a regular set of doubles using this method.

114—MONKEY IN THE MIDDLE

Objective
This entertaining and challenging drill helps players learn how to keep shots away from the middle of the court and builds net-playing skills.

Description
This drill can be performed with as few as three players or as many as six. By keeping their shots away from the net player (monkey in the middle), players develop sound crosscourt and down-the-line rallying skills. The drill forces players to move the ball around the center of the court or suffer the consequences.

Execution
With six players on the court, two players are positioned at each baseline and two are up at net standing opposite each other. A server feeds the ball into play. The four backcourt players rally for points, trying to prevent the net players (monkeys) from snatching the volley away. When a net player steals or poaches on three balls and wins the point, that side of the net rotates so that one of the baseline players gets a chance to play up at the net.

Tip
Players should use the lob to open up the forecourt instead of trying to blast the ball through the net players.

chapter 10

Court-Surface Tactics

Playing on different court surfaces can be either a lot of fun or extremely frustrating. The experience can be maddening to players who don't change their tactics slightly. Tennis courts around the world have changed and improved right along with the game. Players used to find court surfaces that ranged from cow manure to red rippled rubber courts, but most tennis today is played on four types of surfaces: hard, grass, Har-Tru, clay, and red clay.

To perform and play their best on hard courts, players must expect a fast-paced, hard, and grueling game in which first serves are important and aggressive returns are the name of the game. To play on softer courts like grass, players have to be ready for bad bounces and slippery footing. People have described grass as a tricky or even wicked surface to play on. Players who have dreamed of playing on grass must be ready for some fast-paced quick-foot drilling to prepare for this unforgiving surface. In contrast, clay or Har-Tru are slow court surfaces. Patience, consistency, and using a combination of shots are key on Har-Tru and clay. To become suave clay- or Har-Tru-court masters, players must possess an endless supply of patience and oxygen. They must become literally like a backboard in that they can never miss.

Whatever the court surface, players must be ready to adapt and adjust their game plan. This chapter deals with how to adapt playing styles to compete successfully on all tennis court surfaces.

115—FIVE-BALL RECOVERY

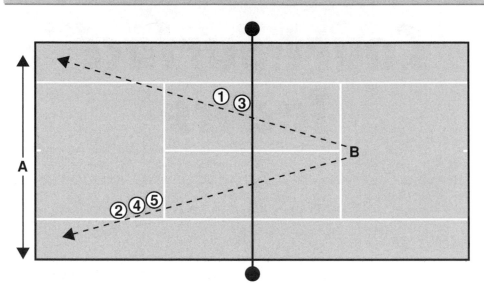

Objective

This drill focuses on quick change of direction and recovery while playing on clay and Har-Tru courts.

Description

Hitting behind the opponent is a wonderful tactic for players to have in their repertoire. The idea is to get the opponent running in one direction and then hit to the area he or she just left. On clay or Har-Tru the player will have a hard time getting enough traction to reverse direction quickly.

Execution

Player A is positioned behind the baseline at the center (T). Player B is positioned up at the net on the opposite side. Player B feeds a sequence of four shots, moving player A from corner to corner hitting forehands and backhands. On the fifth feed player B sends the ball back to the place that player A just left. This method is called hitting behind a player. Players repeat the drill until they gain a firm grasp on how to perform a quick change of direction and recover with good balance. Of course, they should be on a clay court. Scoring is optional.

Tip

Sliding into shots is not only fun but smart. An important tip is to keep the front foot pointed somewhat into the direction of the slide. The back foot can be sideways because it will skip over any catches in the clay or Har-Tru surface instead of being jammed into them.

116—SERVE AND APPROACH LOW

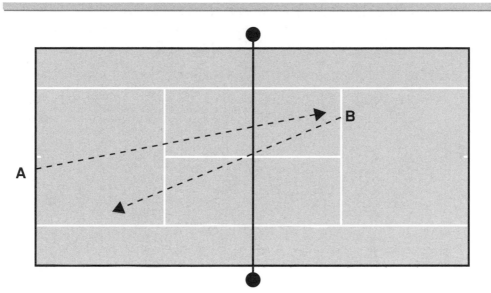

Objective

This drill focuses on serving with added spin to keep the ball lower and hitting low, controlled approach shots while playing on Har-Tru and clay.

Description

Players should expect to need better serves and approach shots for success at the net while playing on Har-Tru and clay. Opponents will have more time to set up on passing shots or lobs, and players will have less traction to make sudden cuts toward the ball. Serve-and-volley players typically have a tough time on clay and Har-Tru courts.

Execution

Player A is positioned at the baseline center (T), and player B receives the serve from the deuce court on the opposite side of the net. Player A hits predetermined slice serves to player B. Player B returns the serve crosscourt, and the players play out the point. When a short ball arises, the player who receives it should move in and hit an approach shot down the middle or down the line with lots of slice or backspin, trying to keep the ball low. Players should play out the point. They play games of 11 points and switch positions after each game.

Tip

Clay and Har-Tru courts are great equalizers. Big servers sometimes find themselves neutralized by the slow surface so they should work on placement rather than power.

117—TRACTION AND BALANCE

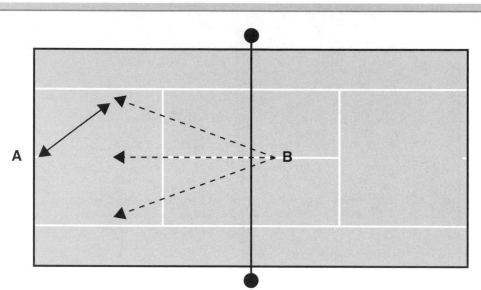

Objective

This drill helps clay-court and Har-Tru players develop better traction and balance for playing on clay.

Description

This simple but vitally important drill helps players learn how to run down the ball on clay and Har-Tru, slide into the ball, and recover to hit the return shot. By having to respond to quick feeds in all directions on the court, players develop the muscles they need to dig into the clay and Har-Tru courts, hold their balance, and change direction as fast as they can on hard courts.

Execution

Player A takes a position at the baseline near the center (T). Player B is up at the net on the opposite side armed with a basket of balls. Player B hits a series of random shots to player A. Player A must run to return the shots to player B and then return to the center (T) after each shot. Player B can hit a predetermined number of shots or continue until player A faints.

Tip

Because opponents will be able to retrieve shots more easily, hitting with pace and accuracy is important to hitting winners on clay. Slice helps keep the ball low to the ground and determines whether or not an opponent is physically fit enough to play on clay. Players should exploit the drop shot and the lob and watch the opponent slip, slide, and hustle to recover their strategically-placed shots.

118—HURRICANE

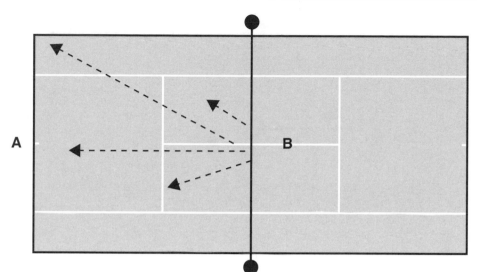

Objective

This drill builds stamina for playing on Har-Tru and helps clay-court players learn how to change directions quickly, keep good balance, and place shots effectively.

Description

This drill works to improve players' stamina through running short distances with quick bursts of speed to recover shots hit randomly around the court. During most clay-court or Har-Tru-court matches, points take a long time to complete. Outright winners are virtually nonexistent, so players can expect at least a 10- to 15-ball exchange.

Execution

Player A is positioned on the baseline at the center (T). Player B or a server is up at the net on the opposite side. Player B hits a series of random shots to player A around the singles court. Player A may hit anywhere within the singles-court area but must hit each ball on the first bounce. If player A misses a shot or lets the ball bounce more than once, he or she must keep attempting to hit the same shot until a successful shot results. Player B or the server should make the balls challenging but not out of reach of player A. Player A must stay on the court until he or she completes all shots.

Variation

The baseliner can attempt to hit 10 balls in a row. For every ball missed, a point is deducted. For example, player A hits balls 1, 2, 3, and 4 over but mis-hits ball 5. The player must then start from ball 4. If the player mis-hits ball 4, he or she starts from ball 3 and so on.

Tip

Slice is the most effective spin players can use on clay and Har-Tru.

119—MAD BATTER

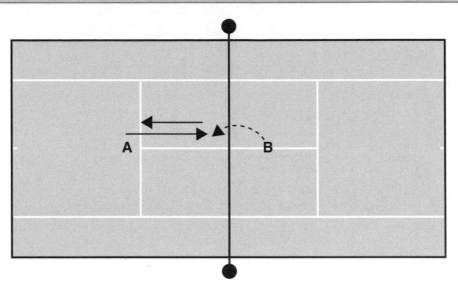

Objective

This tough conditioning drill develops quick feet and quick hands for clay-court and Har-Tru-court tennis.

Description

Players are required to hit drop shots and recover in time to hit another shot before it bounces twice. Traction and stamina are important with this killer drill. Players who can complete two minutes of this drill will not only be able to handle clay and Har-Tru but also will be in phenomenal shape.

Execution

Player A is positioned on the service line, and player B is positioned up at the net on the opposite side. Player B feeds player A a soft ball that drops just in front of the net on player A's side. Player A must run up and hit a drop shot anywhere on the opposite side of the net and then backpedal and touch the service line (T) with the racket. Player B feeds a sequence of soft shots for a two-minute period. Player A continues to run up, hit a drop shot, and back-pedal to the service line (T), touching it with the racket each time until he or she completes two minutes. Players should switch positions after each two-minute period.

Tip

If players are still learning how to hit the drop shot, they aren't yet able to disguise it fully. They should limit their use of the drop shot during competition until they have mastered it and opponents can't read when it's coming.

120—FAST GRASS

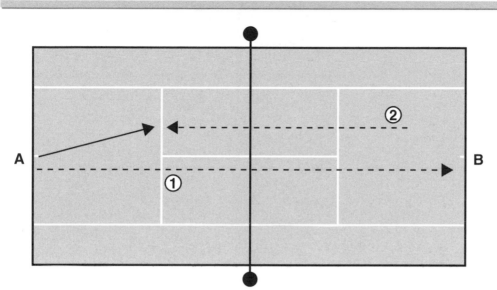

Objective

This drill helps players develop a sound serve-and-attack game for fast surfaces.

Description

A grass surface forces players to play perfect tennis. Players must place their serves, hit stinging, meaningful returns, and keep their minds focused two strokes ahead of the present. On this surface, rallies are scarce but incredibly exciting when they occur.

Execution

Players A and B are positioned at opposite baselines. Player A begins the rally with a drop feed to player B. The players rally until one player hits a shot inside one of the service boxes. The player who received the short shot must attack the shot and close in on the net. Both players can be up at the net at the same time. The goal of this drill is to keep the ball deep in the opponent's court so that he or she will never have the chance to come to the net to hit a winning shot.

Tip

A dry court is radically different from a damp one. The footing will change, as will the strokes. For that reason, players at Wimbledon must adapt their strategies as they get closer to the final rounds. The courts are drier and harder, so players must come up with strokes that shorten the rallies.

121—MAKE IT OR BREAK IT

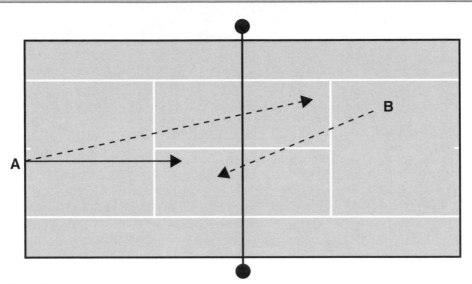

Objective

This drill works serve and return placement, quick reaction to the ball, rapid change of direction, footwork, and recovery skills.

Description

The serve and return of serve are players' bread-and-butter shots on grass. The better the ball placement, the better the chance of winning the point. Most players play around the issues of placement, depth, and pace (speed and spin). The goal is to keep the opponent guessing. On the return, players seek to keep the incoming attacker off balance.

Execution

Player A takes a position behind the baseline at the center (T) in the service ready position. Player B takes a position behind the deuce service court, the court to the right. Player A starts the point by serving and approaching the net to hit a volley away from player B. Player B tries to hit the return at player A's feet or pass down the line. Players play out the point. The first to win 21 points wins the match. Players should rotate after the first set of 21 points.

Variation

Players can play an entire match trying to serve and volley.

Tip

The returner should focus most of the returns down at the feet of the serve and volleyer. This approach will cause the server to volley the shot up and gives the returner prime opportunity to move in and smack a winner.

122—RETURN OF THE BIG SERVE

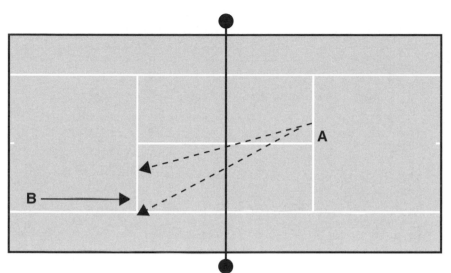

Objective
This drill develops quick reactions to fast serves, quick feet, a compact back-swing, and a pronounced forward attack.

Description
This unique drill can be intimidating at first, but with continuous effort the player who returns will start to develop better footwork, quicker reflexes, and confidence in returning powerful serves.

Execution
Player A, positioned up at the service line, serves to player B. Player B, positioned at the baseline behind one of the service boxes, must try to react quickly enough to handle the serve. Player B should try to return using all four stances and work on returning the ball with topspin or slice. All returns should hit a targeted area either crosscourt deep or down the line deep in the corner.

Variation
After the returner starts to attack every serve using all the hitting stances, the server should start backing up two feet at a time until he or she reaches the baseline, while continuing to serve. The server should alternate sides of the court from the deuce court to the advantage court and practice the same techniques. Players rotate positions after several minutes.

Tip
Split stepping is essential to reacting quickly and catching the ball out in front of the body.

123—FOUR-HIT SERVE AND VOLLEY

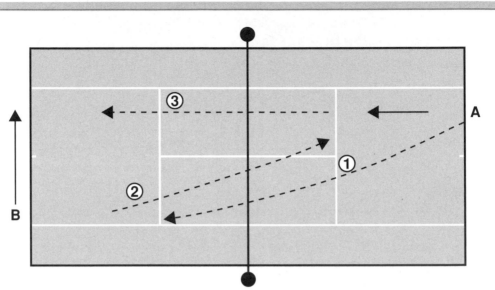

Objective

This drill develops a strong, reliable rhythmic serve and volley, split step, and diagonally forward movement to the volley.

Description

The serve and volley is a key strategy for playing hard-court and grass-court tennis. Practicing this drill will help players create new dimensions in their game and develop sound offensive singles tactics.

Execution

Player A serves into the deuce court, the court to the right of the receiver. Player B, positioned on the opposite side of the court, returns the ball so that player A can follow his or her serve up to the net and volley into the advantage court, the court to the left. Player B shifts over to cover the shot and attempts the passing shot. The players repeat the sequence, with player A serving into the advantage court. Players should rotate after several minutes.

Variation

After players have rotated and practiced in both positions, they play out the points. After one of the players hits the fourth ball in the sequence of shots, the point starts. If the players miss any of the balls during the four-ball sequence, play must start over until the players execute all four patterned balls. They play 11- or 21-point matches, rotating service after every two points.

Tip

Players should think of attacking the net more often when the court surface is fast, the wind is at their back, and they feel their presence at the net may put tremendous pressure on their opponent and cause him or her to make an error.

124—HOT-PEPPER SINGLES

Objective
This entertaining drill helps players develop stamina, net-coverage ability, reflexes, footwork, and confidence when facing fiery action up at the net.

Description
To be effective at the net, players must have excellent reflexes and volleying skills. This drill forces players to stay in the frying pan without backing out. Players will build the confidence they need to keep attacking. Players whose reflexes are quick enough can ultimately rule the net.

Execution
Players A and B face each other standing within the service boxes and straddling the center service line. Player A begins a volley exchange by hitting the ball underhand to player B. The exchange continues until a player makes an error, hits a winning volley, or successfully hits a lob volley over the opponent. Players may not hit outright hard winners at the opponent, and play must start inside the service-court area. They play to 15 or 21 points.

Variation
The point starts after players execute a three-ball exchange. They play forehand-to-forehand volleys only or backhand-to-backhand volleys only.

125—ADVANCED SINGLES HUSTLE

Objective
This drill helps players learn how to hustle for a variety of shots on the court, helps players develop staying ability on the court, and improves confidence.

Description
This drill builds stamina for those long points and teaches players how to run down and cover a variety of shots while playing singles.

Execution
Players position themselves behind the baseline standing in single file with their feet moving (jogging in place). The first player steps up to the center (T) of the baseline. The waiting players move back against the fence or curtain while still moving their feet. A server feeds balls to the first player, making the player hustle for each shot. The server feeds 20 shots—forehands, backhands, drop shots, lobs, short shots, and so on. The level of difficulty should increase for each shot. No scoring is involved.

Variation
Two players hustle to hit and recover all kinds of shots as a team.

126—THREE-HIT BASELINE

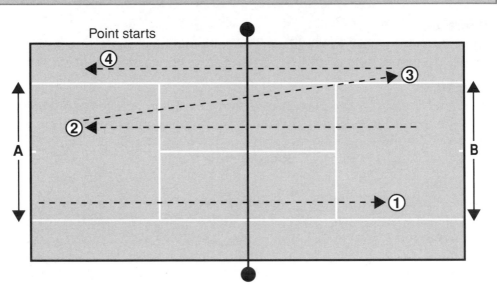

Point starts

Objective
This drill builds ground-stroke consistency, placement of shots, footwork, and recovery skills.

Description
The drill calls for two players at opposite ends of the court. The challenge is to keep many balls in play to build ground-stroking consistency and confidence in placing different types of shots.

Execution
This baseline drill begins with a drop-hit ground-stroke serve. Player A feeds a drop-hit serve deep in the backcourt to player B. The ball must pass over the net three times before the point starts. Players do not volley within the first three hits. They play 11 or 15 points.

Variation
The drill can be done as a doubles drill, and players can adjust the number of times the ball must pass over the net before the point starts.

Tip
Hard-court tennis is quick, powerful, and exciting. Players should work on their consistency, depth, spin, and speed. Their reflexes must be on, and they must have timing and confidence.

127—FOUR-HIT PASSING SHOT

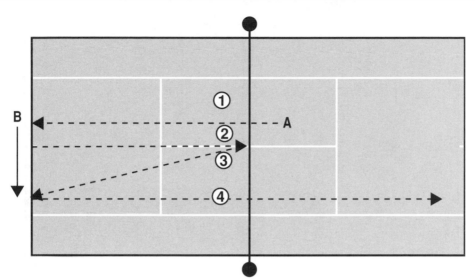

Objective

This drill helps players develop quick thinking skills while hitting passing shots on the run.

Description

To play good hard-court tennis, players must improve their overall conditioning, quicken their footwork, and develop consistency, agility, and anticipation skills. This drill helps players stay steady while running down shots by improving their placement and footwork while hitting on the run and recovering.

Execution

Player A, at the net on one side of the court with a basket of balls, puts the first ball into play by hitting it down the line. Player B returns the ball to player A, who then volleys the ball crosscourt to a target (a prepositioned cone or marker). Player B runs and attempts to hit a passing shot down the line past player A. Player A then slides over to the other side of the court and repeats the steps. Players switch positions after every few points.

Variation

Players rotate to different positions after playing three to five points.

Tip

Players should angle their volleys 99 percent of the time. Volleys hit down the middle of the court tend to come back as winners for the opposing player.

128—TWO-ON-ONE SERVE AND VOLLEY

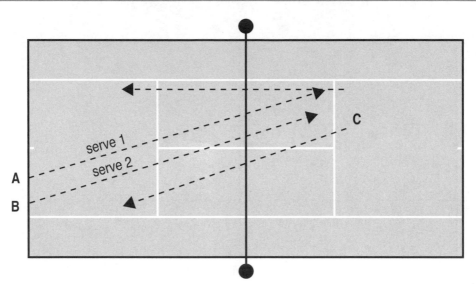

Objective

This drill helps players improve their serve-and-volley tactics, finish off points on hard or grass courts in less time, improve footwork, and develop quick reaction to the ball and rapid advancement to the net.

Description

The drill works the techniques needed to execute the serve volley effectively, and it gives players the opportunity to work on the serve-and-volley game while playing out points.

Execution

Players A and B, who are both positioned behind the baseline, alternate serves to player C. Player C, positioned behind either the deuce or advantage service box, returns the serves. The servers should use only second serves (second serves tend to have more spin and are slower so the returner can more easily return the ball). Player C can use either the chip and charge or the drive when returning the ball. The first player to accumulate 11 points wins. Players should rotate positions.

Tip

Hard-court tennis is hard to master and extremely hard on the body. The surface doesn't allow players unlimited years of comfortable, injury-free play. Players should have an alternative game plan that allows them to end points in fewer than six shots.

chapter 11

Mental Mechanics

It's all about attitude! At one time I didn't know this, but after more than 30 years of playing tennis, I understand why my father, my coach, and now my students wonder why competing and winning seem to come naturally to me, while others play their best matches only on the practice court.

Controlling mental attitude is as important to players as improving their ground strokes and physical conditioning. Mental attitude is often the distinguishing factor between winning and losing in closely contested matches. Although ever-changing external factors can influence players, they can change their mental attitude at will by understanding how to do it.

I had the luxury of learning mental conditioning at an early age. From the moment I picked up a racket at age four, my coaches taught me how to be resolute, how to focus and visualize, how to control my temper, and how to respect the game, my opponent, and myself. They taught me that each point in a match is important and that I might lose a close match if my mind starts to drift for a couple of points. They taught me that I could improve my concentration by relaxing and taking my time to execute and complete each point. They taught me how to focus on the next point, how to think of two-shot combinations, and how to play within my capabilities on each shot.

To be mentally tough and mentally prepared, players must learn how to make small changes in the game plan. They should write down a strategy and visualize themselves performing at their ideal level. They should walk with energy, breathe, think, and "relax" from the moment they finish the point until they get ready to play the next. Having a game plan in mind before each point is important. Players should visualize themselves executing the plan before serving or receiving. They must anticipate all shots. Players should take a beat before executing any shot and let go of mistakes as fast as they make them. They should keep intensity high and avoid dragging their feet if they become tired. Breathing deeply and drinking enough water is important. If nerves attack, players can shake out their arms and jump up and down. This action will keep the heart going, which will help players feel that they are in the flow during the match.

Additionally, there is no substitute for scouting the opponent. Players should determine the opponent's strengths—what is his or her favorite shot? Best weapon? Does the opponent display patterns of play? Does he or she serve wide, follow it to the net, and aim the first volley crosscourt? What about tendencies? Does the opponent try to run around that weak backhand to hit a forehand? Players can ask those who may have competed against the player or watched him or her play a match.

Another big help was videotaping my matches. Players should videotape a match and review the tape to watch for negative body language after points they have lost. Negative body language signifies that players are thinking about what has already happened rather than about the next point. Players may want to have a friend use a stopwatch to see how much time they take between points and when changing sides. Do players rush when ahead or behind? Players should remember that they have 25 seconds between points and 90 seconds for changeovers. Against a strong opponent, players should try to make the points, each game, and the match last as long as possible. I learned how to use the extra time to regroup my thoughts and focus on my plan of action for the next point or game. Players should concern themselves with the present and play point for point. They should stay in the moment and try not to think of the past or future. Physical control comes much faster with undivided concentration, so players should never stop concentrating. Self-discipline is vital. Players can get some ideas about maintaining mental well-being during tough matches by watching some of the top pros. What do they do during the time between points? What are their rituals before they serve and return? How do they carry their bodies and rackets as they walk, talk, and play? What about their breathing and the focus of their eyes?

After each match, whether they win or lose, players should remind themselves that at least 90 percent of the process of playing well is the result of mental conditioning and mental attitude. To get past lost points, lost matches, or just ordinary off days, players must find a way to purge their minds of negative thoughts so that they can stay in the game, in the moment. I believe that conditioning mental attitude starts from this moment, from today, and will continue throughout the player's tennis experience.

129—BALL-MACHINE STRETCH VOLLEY

Objective

The purpose of this drill is to improve volleying or ground-stroking skills, footwork, athletic proficiency, quick reaction to the incoming ball, and placement of shots under stress.

Description

Working with a ball machine is challenging both mentally and physically. The ball machine never misses! Because players can set up the ball machine to send balls anywhere on the court, they can isolate and work on a specific stroke or series of strokes as long as they desire without having to stop and start because of a partner's rallying mistakes. Ball-machine drilling helps make any practiced stroke better.

Execution

Players set up the ball machine to feed shots down the line. They position themselves up at the net so that they are ready to hit. The balls coming across the net should simulate the shots of a baseliner trying to pass his or her opponent. After having some success with this drill, players will be able to reach anything that even the best opponents will throw at them. Players who win this drill should let me know!

Variation

Players can use the ball machine to drill any stroke—volleys, overheads, short shots, lobs, forehands, and backhands, from the net to the baseline. Take advantage of this! For example, set the ball to work on ground-stroke patterns like the two-to-one pattern. Players will hit two forehands crosscourt and one backhand crosscourt. Or, try the three-to-one pattern, so players hit three forehands crosscourt and one backhand crosscourt.

The ball machine can also be set to help players learn how to retrieve drop shots and lobs. Set the ball machine to shoot one soft ball, which should land inside of the service-court area, and one hard high shot, which should drive a player back to the baseline to retrieve the lob.

Tip

When using ball machines, keep the playing court clear of loose balls so players can focus on the oncoming ball. Obviously, the ball machine will continue to shoot balls out and in the players' direction whether they look for them or not, so remind your players to keep their eyes peeled and focused on the action at hand—the ball machine never misses.

130—TICK-TOCK

Objective

This drill teaches players, through use of rhythmic patterns, how to set up strategic patterns for placement of shots in singles play. Focusing on patterns also helps players concentrate on their game.

Description

Good athletes make play of their sport look like dance. To make shots look as smooth as silk, players must use rhythmic patterns to develop rallying strategies.

Execution

Player A is positioned on the baseline at the center (T), and player B is positioned on the opposite baseline. Player A begins the rally with a drop-hit serve. Both players work the first pattern. Player A hits one shot crosscourt and the next down the line. Player B does the same. The players use each pattern of hitting for at least 10 minutes before trying the next. Player A hits three shots crosscourt and the next one down the line. Player B does the same. They practice this pattern for at least 10 minutes. Tick-tock, tick-tock stands for a crosscourt, down-the-line, crosscourt, down-the-line pattern. Tick-tick-tick-tock stands for three shots crosscourt and then one shot down the line. Pattern development will help players concentrate more on the game plan than on whom they are playing.

Variation

Players can mix up tick-tock rhythmic patterns. Using cue words such as "bounce-hit" when drilling or playing can help develop concentration skills. A cue word is one that players say to themselves or one that the coach says repeatedly to players while they are working to achieve a certain task. It may sound silly, but it really works.

Tip

Players should remember to keep their head steady or still like a golfer through contact. One overlooked leading cause of a mis-hit ground stroke is slight lifting of the chin or head just before connecting with the ball. This tiny movement changes the angle of the racket face, thereby changing the hitting zone. It can also throw a player off balance. In order for players to drive shots the full length of the court with increased accuracy, they need to learn to trust themselves and keep their head down and eyes focused on the ball through contact, like a golfer.

James "Riley" Blake

The Master of Determination

© Sport The Library

Born in Yonkers, New York; age 22; height six-feet-one; weight 170 pounds; plays right-handed. James began his tennis career at age 5. At age 13 he was told that he had severe scoliosis (curvature of the spine), which forced him to wear a back brace 18 hours a day. But that didn't stop this master of determination from practicing with his brother Thomas and joining some of the tennis clinics at their local tennis club. James had developed a love and determination for tennis that would someday see him holding the number-17 spot on the ATP ranking computer. Blake attended Harvard University and was the top-ranked collegiate player in 1998-99. He was the NCAA Collegiate Player of the Year in 1998-99, won two ATP Challenges in 2000, and became a semifinalist in the Hall of Fame Tennis Championships. Strength, confidence, and determination fuel this player. James has a big heart of gold and great love for the athletes of Special Olympics. He has never stopped reaching for his goal of walking in the footsteps of his mentor, his coach Mr. Brian Barker, and his inspiration, Mr. Arthur Ashe. James believes that the only thing that separates the guy ranked number 1 from the guy ranked number 200 is confidence.

131—THREE-ON-ONE PASSING SHOT

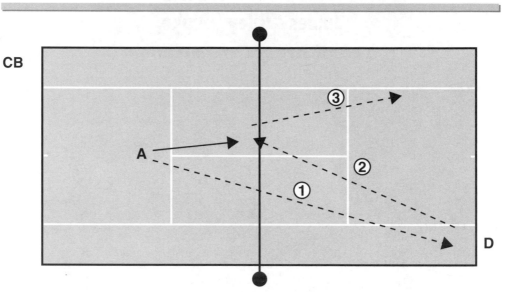

Objective

This drill teaches players how and when to hit approach shots and builds confidence in hitting solid passing shots.

Description

By isolating strokes and patterns, players can practice them so that they become second nature. When players are in match play, patterns of performance should click right in without their having to think about it.

Execution

Player A is positioned up at the net, and player D is positioned on the baseline. Players C and B wait in line to rotate in after one point is played. Player A hits a ball to player D's backhand and approaches the net. Player D hits the passing-shot ball, and player A volleys the ball to the other side of the court. Players C and B repeat the pattern several times to the same side of the court. Player D rotates after the players have had a chance to play. Scoring is optional because this is a practice drill.

Variation

Different players can rotate to all positions. Players can hit forehands.

Tip

Players should train for good endurance, strength, flexibility, and speed. They should enhance their repertoire of shots and add topspin, slice, lobs, and drop shots and remember that their physical fitness determines their mental toughness.

132—HARDCORE GROUND-STROKE VOLLEY

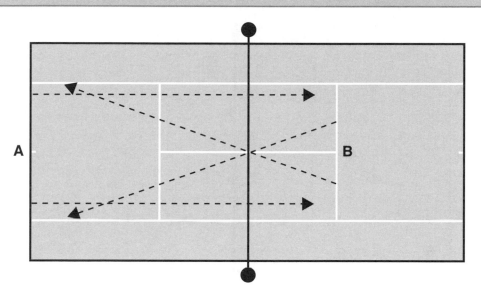

Objective

This drill develops players' control and accuracy in a ground-stroke-to-volley game situation. The drill helps singles players build the confidence they need to run down any shot and get to any volley hit wide or down the line.

Description

This drill keeps players on their toes while teaching them to control the ball, recover quickly after hitting, and maintain a solid hitting pattern while under some stress.

Execution

Player A starts at the baseline, and player B is up at the net. Player A hits every ball down the line, and player B hits every ball crosscourt. After 5 or 10 minutes they switch directions.

Variation

Player A must hit every third ball with a specific stroke and to a specific area on the court. For example, player B hits every volley down the line and player A hits every shot crosscourt, but on the third ball player A hits a crosscourt topspin lob.

Tip

Players can improve their ball control if they learn to obey their on-court "speed limit." Players' speed limit on the tennis court is the maximum pace they can put on the ball without losing control of it. By limiting the speed, players will improve placement and consistency and will become better and stronger players.

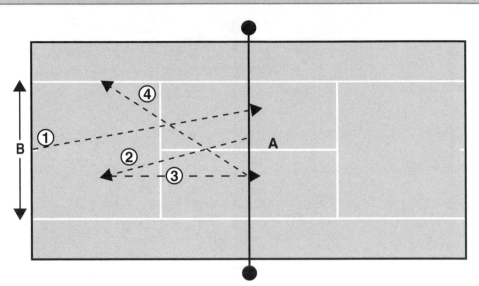

Objective

This drill develops players' confidence in hitting passing shots when on the run and when tired.

Description

The drill helps players learn to hit to a certain area of the court when tired or on the run. Players will learn how to perform and carry out the game plan even when they would rather be lying on the ground.

Execution

Player A is positioned up at the net on one side of the court, and player B is positioned behind the baseline on the opposite side of the net. Player B must return all balls to player A's side of the court. Player A volleys them back to just barely within reach of player B. The intention is to get player B to run as much as possible for each ball but at the same time keep the ball in play for as long as possible. Scoring is optional because this is a practice drill. Players rotate positions after several minutes.

Tip

When hitting a ball and running at full speed, players must keep the eyes focused on the incoming shot and keep the head steady. If they try to peek at the shot, they will mis-hit the ball or the shot won't make it past the service line on their side of the court.

134—TWO BACK-ONE UP

Objective
This drill teaches quick recovery skills, liability of short volleys, passing-shot coverage, quick feet and hands, and anticipation skills.

Description
The drill challenges a net player's game. By having two players positioned on the baseline to challenge the net player, the drill forces the net player to work hard and think clearly so that he or she can move quickly enough to cover every shot.

Execution
Two players position themselves behind the baseline, one on the deuce side (the service court to the player's right when facing the service-court area), and the other on the advantage side (the service court to the left). One player is up at the net on the opposite side of the net. The baseliners hit shots at the net player and try to move him or her around as much as possible. The backcourt players should hit lobs and mix in some passing shots. All balls should be within reach of the net player. Scoring is optional.

Tip
The backcourt players should use a variety of lobs, topspin, and backspin and hit high and deep or with bullet trajectory. They can mix in some soft passing shots as well.

135—SHADOW VOLLEY

Objective
This drill teaches players proper footwork while volleying in a simulated point-playing situation.

Description
This entertaining drill helps players learn to watch the ball, set up points, and anticipate shots.

Execution
Players separate into two lines behind the service-line center on opposite sides of the court. Players volley against each other until one player misses or the ball bounces. They must hit all shots as volleys and keep the ball inside their respective service-box areas. The first team to accumulate 11 or 15 points wins.

Variation
Players can be limited to using only their forehand volleys or only their backhand volleys. If players are restricted to use of the forehand volley, a shot hit with the backhand volley ends the point. This rule forces players to use their feet and strategically figure out how to hit to the opposing team's wrong side.

136—EVERLASTING SERVICE

Objective
Eliminating the second serve forces players to concentrate on executing good ball tosses, spin serves, and excellent placement of serve while under pressure.

Description
This drill helps players develop good concentration skills while trying to hold or break service games.

Execution
Player A serves game after game until player B breaks serve. If player A fails to win two or three games before player B breaks serve, player B takes over the service game. Players can execute this method while playing an entire match.

Tip
Players should work on consistency and be patient while building the point.

137—CAPTAIN HOOK SERVICE

Objective
This drill develops consistency and effectiveness of second serves. The second serve must be as reliable as the rising of the sun.

Description
This drill helps players develop a reliable second serve by allowing only one serve per point.

Execution
In a set or match of singles or doubles, players are allowed only one serve per point. They lose the point if the server misses the serve.

Variation
Players should incorporate the one-serve-only rule while playing a 15-point game or a 12-point tiebreaker. These mental tactics should really challenge your service fortitude while under pressure.

Tip
The server should concentrate on using second serves and placement. The second serve should have a lot more spin and less pace.

138—PREPLANNED SET

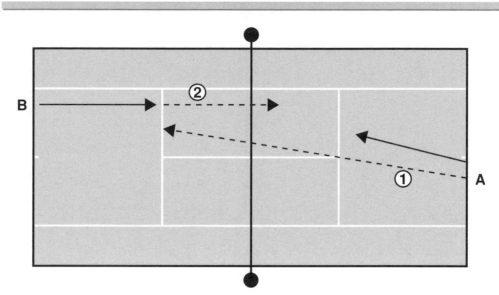

Objective

Playing with preplanned formulas isolates a specific area of the game. By practicing any combination of shots using this method, players build confidence for match-play situations.

Description

Players play an entire set aiming the serve and return to a specific area. Players practice one predetermined pattern to help make the sequence of strokes second nature.

Execution

Player A serves every ball to player B's backhand, and player B returns every ball to A's backhand volley. Only serves and returns are predetermined; all other shots are up to the players. After the return, players play out the point as usual, using regular scoring. Players may use this method to play an entire match or just to practice a few points. As players run this pattern, they start to imprint it in their minds for future match play.

Variation

Players can use any preplanned configuration of serve and return of serve.

Tip

Anticipation, like the killer instinct, is an art learned through many hours of practice and playing hundreds or thousands of points, games, and matches. You can't buy it or find it.

139—VOLLEY LUNGE

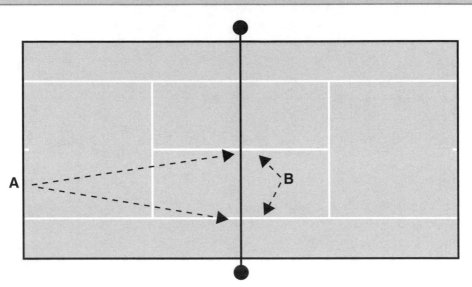

Objective

This challenging drill develops stamina, quick evasive movements, quick recovery, and anticipation skills.

Description

This drill develops sound volleying technique, helps players avoid swinging up at the net, forces players to keep the racket out in front, and allows players to let the racket do most of the work.

Execution

Player A stands to the right of the center (T) at the baseline. Player B stands up at the net inside of one of the service boxes, either deuce or advantage. Player A hits a ball wide to player B down the alley sideline. Player B returns the shot with a volley back to player A. Player A hits the ball wide crosscourt back to player B. Player B returns the shot with a volley back to player A. They repeat this sequence a few times and then switch positions.

Tip

If players have a tendency to hit volleys into the net, they may be stopping the forward movement of the racket. This action causes the racket head to dump over slightly, which sends the ball down into the net. Another problem is releasing the tension in the wrist and allowing the racket head to drop out sideways below the wrist. Players should try to keep moving as they approach the volley to ensure a solid hit. When stretched out wide to hit a passing-shot volley, they should always keep the wrist cocked high.

140—SERVE AND VOLLEY

Objective

This drill isolates one aspect of an aggressive game plan, the serve and volley. The drill develops quick feet and hands, anticipation skills, and ability to close in on the net.

Description

By practicing only the serve-and-volley tactic, players can work specifically on the footwork, reflexes, and confidence they need to use this plan during match play.

Execution

Player A is behind one of the service boxes and hits returns, while players B, C, and D serve and volley from behind the opposite baseline. Servers alternate playing out points against the receiver. The first player who wins 10 points, either the receiver or one of the serve and volleyers, wins the drill.

Variation

Servers are allowed only one serve and must close in and volley or forfeit the point and turn. The receiver must hit returns to a designated area of the court (down the line, down the middle of the court, or a chip low at the server's feet).

141—HARA-KIRI AT THE NET

Objective

This drill helps players learn how to move out wide for volleys and recover quickly with control. The drill also helps build agility, speed, and confidence in total court coverage.

Description

By exhausting the primary player, this drill helps him or her become a more physically and mentally balanced player. After performing this drill numerous times, players will think that running down shots or leaping for shots during match play is a piece of cake.

Execution

Players A and B position themselves on the baseline, and player C, the primary player in this drill, takes a position up at the net. Players A and B feed balls from the backcourt in such a way that player C must lunge from alley to alley to make the volleys. Players switch after several minutes.

Variation

Players set up the same way except that player C starts at the center of the opposite baseline. Players A and B are positioned up at the net and feed balls to player C that force him or her to run but are within reach. The purpose is to run player C from side to side and up and back. Player C must return the ball.

142—PATTERNED NET RUSH

Objective

This drill isolates a game plan for attack and recovery at the net. The drill enhances midcourt and net coverage, quick footwork, development of net confidence, and anticipation. Players build overall knowledge of what to do in common situations in singles match play.

Description

During match play, players must perform extremely fast-paced exchanges of volleys at the net. The purpose of this drill is for players to practice those fast volleys in a programmed fashion to solidify the techniques they need to perform effectively under stress.

Execution

After announcing where the serve will land, player A serves and volleys to player B. Player B returns the serve to player A. Player A makes a first volley back to player B. Player B lobs the ball over player A, and player A hits an overhead. For both players to benefit, at least five shots must go over the net and in the court within reach of the opponent. Players must keep the first five balls in play. From the sixth ball on, both players may try to win points.

Variation

The server should serve to different areas, and the receiver should return to both sides to vary the pattern.

143—SCRAMBLED EGG

Objective

This drill improves confidence, speed, conditioning, and agility at the net.

Description

The drill helps players develop the speed, agility, confidence, and fundamental technique they need to hit any shot they may encounter up at the net during competition.

Execution

Player A serves and attacks the net. Player B, who is on the opposite side of the court, disregards the served ball and proceeds to hit a sequence of 20 different shots from a nearby basket of balls. Player B should watch for loose balls rolling around under player A's feet. The object is to make player A hit the first volley and move quickly from side to side and up and back for difficult drives, lobs, and fluff balls. After completing a sequence of 20, players switch positions or rotate. No scoring is involved.

PART

Competition and Match Play

This part of *The Tennis Drill Book* is dedicated to all tennis players who love to play, want desperately to improve their skills, but hate drilling. Players can accomplish monumental changes in their tennis-playing skills by playing exciting competitive tennis games. Competitive tennis games are a combination of strategic drills and entertaining games. So while players are having fun— laughing, huffing and puffing, playing king or queen of the court—they are also learning how to move, focus, and think like competitive singles players. No, it's not sneaky, it's just another way of keeping tennis fun.

While practicing their fundamentals through competitive game playing, players are essentially working toward the goal of becoming better and smarter players. For example, if players need to improve their ground-stroking consistency, they can play a regular game of tennis except that any ground stroke hit in the net automatically loses the entire game. Wouldn't that motivate players to keep the ball in play? How about if a player has volleying jitters and just hates to play the net or just doesn't know when to approach the net? That player can play a regular game of tennis except that the only way to win a point is up at the net with a volley or overhead. Reinforcing tennis fundamentals doesn't always require constant drilling, nor should it. A better approach is playing competitive singles games.

chapter 12

Singles Games

Playing competitive singles games is the best way to reinforce what a player learns through practice drills. Practicing by playing competitive games helps players, both adults and children, stay excited about learning tennis. Drills are routines that allow players to hit a large number of balls to reinforce proper strokes, groove their shots, and practice situations that occur during competition, but games help a player recognize if all the drilling is really paying off. Competitive game playing allows identification of any small progression in a players' game development. Players will be able to see if they really understand the fundamentals of tennis.

Players can grow while competing in fun-filled, creative competitive games that simulate singles-match play. A key ingredient in becoming a successful player is determination. Determination helps create champions on the tennis court and in life. Playing the creative competitive singles games in this chapter will guide players in keeping a positive attitude, whether winning or losing, and competing at all levels of match-play competition. The games will also help players learn the art of competing mentally and physically under pressure while still enjoying the competition. So players should liven up their practice sessions with creative competitive games!

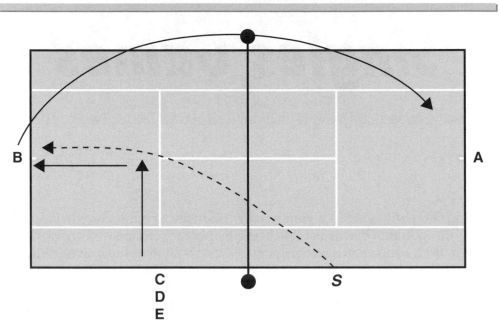

Objective

This game promotes good footwork and teaches players how to play defensive and offensive singles.

Description

This game is King of the Court with a twist. By taking positions next to the doubles sideline at the service line, players learn good footwork, realize the value of early racket preparation, and have fun while learning to keep the ball in play.

Execution

One player takes a position on the opposite side of the court on the baseline and is dubbed the king or queen (tea). The other players (biscuits) line up one behind another next to the doubles sideline at the service line on the opposite side of the court. The server gives the "Go" command, and the first player in line sidesteps out to the center service line (T) and then backpedals to the baseline. At this point the server feeds a forehand ball to the challenger (biscuit). The players begin rallying until one misses. If the challenger wins the point, he or she has five seconds to run from the baseline over to the other baseline, while the next player standing in line sidesteps out to the service line (T) and backpedals to the baseline. If the king or queen wins the point, he or she keeps the point and remains king or queen. The challenger goes to the end of the line. The first player to win 15 points wins the game.

145—KING OR QUEEN OF THE COURT GAME

Objective
This game helps players of any level improve their singles skills in a fun, mildly pressured game situation.

Description
The game allows players to test their consistency, ball-placement skills, and singles strategy while competing in a singles match-play situation.

Execution
One player, the king or queen, takes the top position on the opposite side of the court from the challengers. The challengers are positioned off the court and take turns playing out points against the king or queen to try to take over the top position. After accumulating a certain number of points, perhaps 10, the challenger dethrones the king or queen and takes over the top position of the court. Only the challenger collects points. The king or queen works only to play out the points to prevent the challenger from dethroning him or her. All the other players lose their points and must start from zero.

Variation
This game can be played in the minicourt area as well. Players can play king or queen doubles.

146—ROTATING SINGLES GAME

Objective
This game reinforces ground-stroking skills, footwork, and ball placement.

Description
Players learn how to build up points to move in and attack to win the point.

Execution
Rotating singles is like OUT singles (see chapter 13) except that after hitting the first ball, players rotate to the end of the line on their side of the court only. Players A and B take positions behind one baseline center (T), and players C and D take positions behind the opposite baseline center (T). The doubles alleys are out. The server feeds the first ball to player A, who hits a ground stroke to player C. Player A rotates to the end of the line, and player B steps in to receive the shot coming back from player C. Player C hits player A's shot and rotates to the end of the line, and player D steps up to receive the shot that player B will hit. Players hit and rotate until the point ends. The first team to win 21 points wins the match.

Tip
This game is a great conditioning tool if players jog in place between hitting the shots.

147—ROTATING CANADIAN SINGLES GAME

Objective

This game helps develop good footwork, strategy, ground-stroking fundamentals, and good gamesmanship.

Description

This game encourages singles strategizing. Playing two against one is hard enough, but incorporating the anything goes rule helps the singles player and doubles players think of creative ways to build and set up shots to win the point or game. This game is important because it is the beginning stage of learning how to think strategically on the tennis court. Singles players must decide how to set up their shot so that they can close in on the net and finish the point fast, or they will literally run out of steam trying to out-rally two players on the opposite side of the net.

Execution

Rotating Canadian singles is the same as one-on-one rotating singles except that two players play against one. Player A takes a position at the opposite side of the court behind the baseline center (T). Player A is king or queen of the court. Other players take positions in teams of two behind the other baseline. The singles player hits into the doubles alleys, but the challenging teams use only the singles-court area. A server feeds the ball to player A, the king or queen, to start. Player A plays out the point against the first team up on the baseline. If the team wins the point, they keep it and continue to play until they either accumulate 15 points and win the match or lose a point. Teams rotate whenever a point is lost. The first team to reach 15 points against the king or queen wins the match.

Variation

Including an additional player to compete against the king or queen adds a level of difficulty for the singles player.

Tip

Players should remember that depth and control are more important than pace. Singles players have quite a bit of court to cover, so playing smarter instead of trying to hit every ball harder is the way to go. Players should be definite about shot selection and court positioning, and work to build up points before unleashing every weapon in their arsenal.

148—TENNIS BLACKJACK GAME

Objective
This game develops ball-placement skills, footwork, and ground-stroking skills.

Description
The game challenges players to use their weaker strokes. By forcing them to hit using a weak stroke, the game encourages players to improve that specific stroke.

Execution
During the game, players may choose to use any stroke that they feel they need to work on—running forehands, backhands, overheads, or whatever. All players are positioned single file behind the baseline center (T). A server is on the opposite side of the court up at the net. The first player in line comes up to the baseline center (T) and attempts to hit the specific stroke. If the player hits the shot into the singles-court area between the net and the service line, he or she receives 1 point. Placing the ball between the service line and the baseline earns 2 points. Players rotate after every shot. If a player accumulates 13 points, he or she loses a turn, forfeits all points, and starts again from zero. The first player to reach 21 points wins.

149—MINI-ME TENNIS GAME

Objective
This game helps develop finesse skills, footwork, and court movement.

Description
The game helps players develop a feel for the ball by isolating the playing area. Players can hit any type of shot and spin with pace or use a little finesse to win points.

Execution
Players are positioned up at the service line opposite each other. Player A starts the game with either a drop feed or by using a regular serve. Players can use any combination of shots. They should try playing an entire match using the service-court area.

Variation
Players can work on their serving and volleying by using the rule that the server can score points only by serving and then volleying.

150—SINGLES ATTACK GAME

Objective
This game reinforces ground-stroking fundamentals, singles strategy, ball placement, and footwork skills.

Description
The game requires players to use all their ground-stroking skills to set up points to attack when the opportunity arises.

Execution
Players A and B are positioned behind opposite baselines. Player A starts the point with either a serve or a drop-hit serve to player B. Both players rally for the point until player B yells, "Attack!" Player A must then rush the net, no matter where the ball is or where player A is. The players try to finish the point. They play to 21 points.

151—SINGLES GO GAME

Objective
This game works on singles strategy, countering overhead smashes, and retrieving lobs.

Description
This fast-paced, exciting game really gets players moving. The game emphasizes lob recovery, overhead placement, and strong baseline recovery skills.

Execution
Players line up behind the baseline. A player dubbed the king or queen is at the net standing on the opposite side. A challenger steps up to the baseline. A server feeds a difficult overhead to the king or queen, who tries to put away the overhead against the first challenger. If the king or queen is successful, he or she stays up at the net, receives one point, and faces another challenger. If the king or queen loses the point, the server yells, "Go!" and the challenger runs from his or her side of the court to the other while the server hits a high difficult lob for the challenger to put into play against the new challenger. If the new king or queen wins the point, he or she starts up at the net. The king or queen who lost goes to the end of the line but keeps his or her points.

Variation
Doubles can be played using the preceding rules.

152—HALF COURTING GAME

Objective

This game helps players develop ball-control skills, footwork skills, ball placement, and direction.

Description

This game requires players to learn how to control where they hit the ball. Isolating strokes and the boundaries of the playing court forces players to really concentrate on improving technique. It helps players to forget about all of the other areas within their game that may need work. Adding a little competitive point play also helps players use the troubled area while under the pressure of match play.

Execution

Players A and B are on opposite baselines. Both players are restricted to using only half the court, including the doubles alley. Players can use the deuce half or the advantage half of the court. Player A serves the ball with a drop-hit serve to player B. The serve should fall behind the service line. Both players play out the point using every stroke they know to win the point. Anything goes. The first player to accumulate 21 points wins the game. Serves rotate every 2 points. Players should play with only three balls to keep loose balls away from the playing area.

Variations

Players can play this game using only the alley, or they can play crosscourt and include the doubles alleys. Another variation is to require the receiver of a short shot to move in, play the approach, and then attack the net. The attacking player can retreat from the net only if lobbed; he or she may then stay back and work the point.

Tip

A simple rule to help players achieve the desired direction of many shots is to know that the racket face controls the direction of the ball. The ball will go in the direction the strings are facing because the ball bounces off the racket at right angles. When the racket face is looking diagonally across the net, the ball will go crosscourt. When the racket face is looking squarely at the net with the strings parallel to the net, the ball will go down the line. Remind players of this rule if they are having trouble controlling where they hit the ball.

153—SINGLES MINEFIELD GAME

Objective

This entertaining gaming method teaches players how to control the ball, direct the ball, and use various strokes to hit to designated targets during match play.

Description

Players play out a regular game of tennis, scoring in the usual manner until one player hits a designated target, for which he or she will be rewarded with extra points or games. This game can be played either full court, half court, or minicourt.

Execution

Players A and B are positioned behind opposite baselines. Players play out a regular tennis match with standard scoring. Three small hoops or targets are placed on each side of the net. Both players try to hit a ball into one of the targets while rallying and playing out a point. A player who hits a target automatically wins the point. Scoring is by the regular scoring method—15, 30, 40, game.

Variations

Target hoops are placed only in service boxes, and points can be won by serving into the target hoops. Another variation is to require players to use only one stroke, perhaps backhand ground strokes or backhand volleys or overheads, to hit targets and score a point or game.

chapter 13

Doubles and Multiplayer Games

Doubles players are smart players. Playing smarter requires fixing certain principles firmly in the mind. The best way to condition the doubles mind is to practice gamelike doubles situations. Drilling allows players to focus on particular weaknesses, but when that approach becomes contrived, players end up performing better on the practice court than they do in match play. Games combine the benefits of match-play simulation with the excitement of actual doubles competition.

Playing various competitive doubles games or multiplayer games helps players discover their specific jobs and responsibilities during a doubles match. A player who knows the specific responsibility at each position can perform with elevated confidence during actual doubles competition. Playing the games in this chapter will help players develop the fundamentals for playing doubles matches effectively and competitively.

154—STICKY SITUATION GAME

Objective
This game develops volleying and lobbing skills.

Description
The game improves confidence during attack and defense in doubles play.

Execution
Team A is positioned on the baseline facing team B, positioned up at the net. A server starts the point by feeding the first ball to team A. Team A tries to hit a deep lob over team B. Team B tries to knock off the lob with an overhead to win the point. If the lob is successful, team B must retrieve the lob and hustle back up to the net. Team A is allowed to lob only; no ground-stroke passing shots are allowed. The first team to win 21 points wins the game.

Tip
Players must remember that doubles is a team game. As a team, players should exploit the lob over their opponents' heads and then attack the net. Many teams fail to attack when the opportunity arises. That failure can prove costly because it's easier to win a point at the net than it is at the baseline. Players can use the lob to open up the forecourt rather than trying to blast the ball through their opponents at the net.

155—OUT GAME

Objective
This entertaining game helps players develop consistency, ball placement, and strategy.

Description
Players split up and take positions behind opposite baselines. Only one ball is in play, and players must keep the ball going back and forth across the net, in the singles court only. The action is almost like juggling one ball among a large group of players.

Execution
OUT can be played with six or more players—the more the better. Players split up and take positions opposite each other, standing in a single-file line behind the baseline center (T). A server feeds a ball to the first player in line on either side of the net. That player hits the ball and runs to the end of the line on the opposite side of the court. The first player in the opposite line returns the ball and runs to the end of the line on the opposite side of the court. Play continues until a player misses. That player receives the letter O. Play resumes. Players who accumulate all letters of the word *OUT* are out of the game and sit in a designated area until the game ends. The last player left wins.

156—MOON-BALL GAME

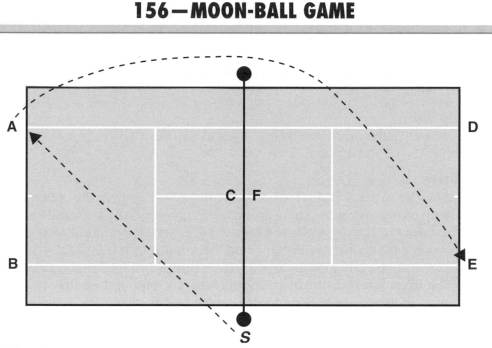

Objective

This game helps players develop lobbing and overhead skills.

Description

Six or more players can play this game. The game teaches players how to lob over their opponents' heads. By isolating the lob and the overhead stroke, players can work out any jitters they have about hitting them during competition.

Execution

Players A, B, and C are a team, and players D, E, and F are a team. Players A and B are on the baseline, and player C is up at the net on the same side. Players D and E are on the opposite baseline, and player F is up at the net on the same side. A server feeds the first ball to player A. The four players at the baseline can hit only lobs. Their goal is to lob over the players at the net so that players C and F can't hit an overhead. Players C and F may not go behind the service line to hit a shot. The players play out the points up to 21 and then rotate so that each team member has a chance to play the net position.

Tip

Weak lobs allow the opposition to move up and smash an overhead for a winner. Players should focus on hitting forward through the ball, apply a little topspin with a low-to-high motion, and complete the follow-through as they would when hitting ground strokes. Players should also try to hit high defensive or offensive lobs with backspin.

157—SURVIVOR GAME

Objective
This game reinforces good stroke production, footwork, shot selection, and ball placement.

Description
The survivor game promotes teamwork and teaches players to think before they hit to avoid setting up themselves or their partners to be killed.

Execution
This game can be played with four or more players—the more the better. Players split up into two groups. There are no teams; players keep their own scores. Players start with 10 lives and lose a life each time they lose a point. One group of players is behind one baseline (T), and the other group is behind the other baseline (T). A server starts the point by feeding a ball to the first player in one of the lines, who hits the ball and rotates to the end of the same line. The first player in the opposite line hits the return and then rotates to the end of that line. The second player in the first line hits this return and rotates. This sequence continues until a player misses and thus loses a life. Players who lose 10 lives sit on the side of the court until the game is over. Play continues until one player remains.

158—FLUB GAME

Objective
This game develops consistency and concentration skills during a heated ball exchange up at the net.

Description
Quick hands and quick feet are the name of this game. When playing doubles, players must be able to react quickly to balls hit straight at them. This game livens up net play so that players will be ready for any ball hit at them or away from them.

Execution
Four players are positioned on the baseline, two on each side of the net. Players begin with 21 points each. Player A puts the ball in play with a serve to player B. Player B returns to player C. Player C returns to player D, and player D returns the ball to player A. Players must not break the sequence of shots. A player who misses a shot loses a point. The player who loses the fewest points wins.

159—KNOCKER TENNIS GAME

Objective

This game helps players determine their skill level and gives them a sense of what it's like to play in a tournament.

Description

Six or more players can participate in this method of match playing. Players of different ability can compete against each other. The rotation of match playing gives each team and player an opportunity to play a variety of match-playing game styles.

Execution

Players should partner up into doubles teams. Teams A, B, C, and D compete against one another. When a team wins a match, they collect 1 point. The team that wins 15 points wins the competition. Each team plays the best of four regular scoring games. The winning team rotates one court up toward the first court, the highest court.

Variation

Players can use this method while playing singles.

Tip

Players should work on building the points slowly and steadily. This approach builds confidence and success on the court. Players should remember the C + A = S equation: Confidence + Aggressiveness = Success.

160—RUSH AND CRUSH GAME

Objective

This game forces players to use their serve-and-volley, passing-shot, and return-of-serve skills.

Description

Players must use their serve-and-volley technique to start the point or they lose the point. The receiving team must use passing shots without lobbing on the first ball.

Execution

Players take standard doubles positions. Team A plays against team B. Team A must serve and volley on both the first and second serves. Team B must return using a passing shot only. After teams use this beginning method they can play out the point in any manner they choose. They play a set using regular scoring methods.

Tip

The receiving team should hit to the feet of the serve and volleyer.

161—SINK OR SWIM GAME

Objective

This game builds doubles-playing techniques and communication.

Description

The game helps players learn how to work as a team. By rewarding one team with a point advantage over the other to start, the players on the defensive team are motivated to fight hard and take advantage of any opportunity to attack.

Execution

Two teams position themselves behind opposite baselines. A server starts the first point by feeding a deep shot to team A. Teams play out the point using doubles strategy. If team A wins the point, they move up to the service line to start the next point. Team B is on the baseline to start. The server feeds another ball to team A to start the point. Teams play out the point. If team B wins this point, team A must backpedal quickly to the baseline and team B starts up on the service line. The server feeds another ball to team A to start the point. If team B wins this point, they move up to the net for their last starting position, and team A starts on the baseline. If team B wins this point, they collect the first game of a 10-game match. The server feeds another ball to team A. If team A wins the point, they move up to the service line, team B backpedals all the way back to the baseline, and the game continues. But if team B wins this point, the first game is over and team B collects the first game of 10. The players switch sides to start another game. The server should feed the first ball to team B.

162—QUICK-CHANGE GAME

Objective

This game method forces players to use all three types of doubles formations—Australian, monster or I formation, and standard.

Description

Players are required to use all three doubles formations during all service games of their match.

Execution

Team A, the serving team, must serve using a different doubles formation to start each point of their service game or they forfeit the game. Team B plays in the standard doubles receiving manner. After team A completes the game, the serve shifts to team B. Team B must serve each point using a different doubles formation or they forfeit the game. The teams play an entire match using this method.

Tip

Good communication between partners is the key to a strong doubles team.

163—TENNIS BASEBALL GAME

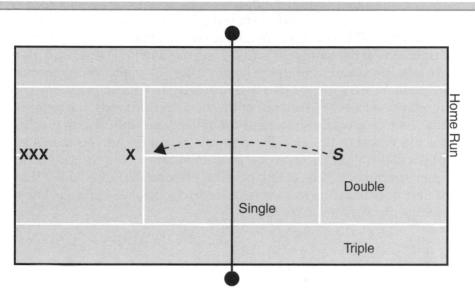

Objective

This game reinforces the value of directing the ball to different areas of the court.

Description

This great game teaches players how to direct and control shots. By using baseball terminology for placement of shots, players get a sense of team participation while practicing ground strokes.

Execution

As few as 2 or as many as 20 players can play tennis baseball. With fewer than 4 players on the court, all players begin on the same side of the court positioned behind the center (T), one behind the other. A server is positioned up at the net and is the pitcher. The first player in line comes up to the baseline (T) or the service line (T), depending on ability level. Each player gets two strikes and then must give up the turn for the next player to step up and hit. Strikes are balls hit into the net, out of the court area, or missed outright. Any ball hit between the net and the service line, which extends into the doubles alley, counts as a single, and the player receives one point. A ball landing inside no-man's land is a double and earns two points. A ball hit into the doubles alley but behind the service line on either side of the court is a triple, worth three points. A ball that hits the baseline on the first bounce is a home run and earns four points. Players keep their own scores. This version of baseball tennis includes no base running, catching, or tagging.

(continued)

Variation

When six or more are playing, the players split up into two teams. One team, team A, takes a position behind the baseline as the hitting team. Team B is in the outfield, the other side of the net, scattered around the court. The net post on the right side of the tennis net is first base, the center (T) is second base, the left net post is third base, and the baseline center (T) on the hitting team's side is home plate. When a hitter hits a ball in a designated area of the court and a fielding player catches the shot out of the air with the hands, the hitter is out. Balls that bounce are safe shots, and the hitter takes the base that coincides with the placement of the shot. For example, a ball hit into no-man's land is a double, and the hitter takes second base. Runs are forced in, and there is no tagging or running from base to base. The placement of the balls hit by the hitter determines the scoring of runs. After three outs, teams rotate. They play nine innings and eat lots of hot dogs!

chapter 14

Match Simulation Games

Tennis players know that pressure is part of competing. The way players perform under pressure will determine if they are going to be serious contenders or just Saturday afternoon social players. If players intend to play club matches or tournaments, they must practice while under pressure to learn how to deal with it in a match. Nothing can substitute for the pressure of actual match-play competition, but specific drills and match-simulated games work as excellent physical and psychological grooving devices. The following section contains some of these situations for players to practice and use during competition. Using these match-simulated drills and games will help players learn how to deal with frustration, setbacks, and winning gracefully.

164—DOUBLES SERVING TEAM GAME

Objective

This drill improves specific team serving strategy and technique. Players learn why and when to use specific strategies and what should happen during match play when they use them.

Description

Players should not only practice drilling specific shots or combination of shots but also practice them in gamelike situations. Playing in gamelike situations helps players adopt the strategies they need to succeed under certain conditions and in certain matches. They play the following situations as the serving team only.

Execution

Players play an eight-game pro set (the player or players must reach eight games and win by a margin of two games). The server must serve and volley on the first and second serves. They practice using signals and poaching on volleys. They should play a 12-point tiebreaker and poach on at least two of every three first serves and on half of the second serves. They play a 12-point tiebreaker using the monster (I) formation on every first serve and on half of the second serves.

Variations

In playing Australian doubles, each player serves four points in the ad court. If the serving team is having a hard time serving and volleying because the receiving team's returns are too difficult, try using the Australian service formation. This formation eliminates the receiving team's crosscourt return. In playing monster doubles, the net player should poach on at least one of the four points. This service formation is a variation of the Australian formation. Players should remind their partner to assume the ready position below the level of the net tape to avoid the risk of getting hit in the back of the head by his or her teammate's serve. Players should also discuss signaling before the start of the match. This aggressive formation really confuses the opposing team, so use it when you need a little extra psychological boost to help control the match.

Tip

The net player should execute a visible body fake (a bluff) when up at net and not moving. A bluff causes opponents to change their original plan of attack when they see the movement. The returner often mis-hits the attempted change of shot or hits it right to the player who used the bluff movement.

165—CHIP-LOB RETURN GAME

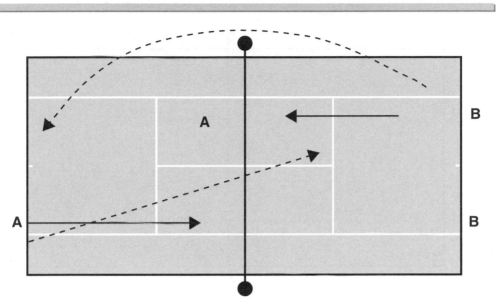

Objective

This game method helps players counter against teams that use the monster (I) doubles formation or just like to poach a lot.

Description

Players can use this method of defense against a team that likes to poach and on second serves. They can use the chip-lob return as a way to get to the net early and force the opposing team to change their game plan.

Execution

Team A is positioned in the monster (I) doubles formation or standard doubles formation. Team B players start back on the baseline. Team A starts the first point of the first game by serving and volleying. Team B must chip lob the return over the net player's head and stay back to work the point. Once team A retreats and scurries back to retrieve the lob, team B should look to attack the net. Both teams continue to play out the point. The teams start each point of each game using this method. Scoring is by the regular system. To reinforce the chip-lob return, teams should play at least three or four sets using this method.

Tip

Players should try to keep the ball in play as long as possible and use high defensive lobs with topspin or backspin.

166—ROTATING DOUBLES GAME

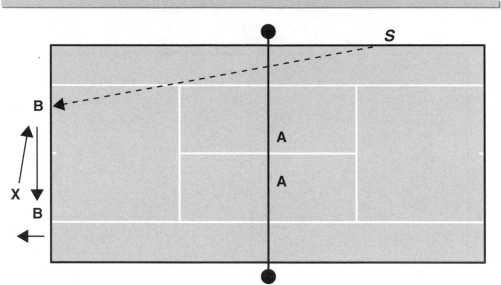

Objective
This game reinforces all aspects of doubles play.

Description
This game helps develop players' various responsibilities during match play.

Execution
Players on team A are at the net as the kings or queens of the court. If five players are playing, two are a team on the opposite baseline. This team must acquire three points consecutively to take over team A's position. A server positioned at the net post feeds the first ball to the player of the challenging team standing behind the deuce court, who has two chances to put the ball in play. If the player misses, he or she rotates over to the advantage side, the player standing behind the advantage court rotates out, and the waiting player moves up to the baseline behind the deuce court. The new challenging team starts with zero points, and a new point begins.

Variation
With an even number of players, teams rotate. Teams must win 3 consecutive points to become the kings or queens. If the challenging team loses a point, a new team rotates in, and the losing team drops all points. When a challenging team accumulates 3 points, they move to the other side and take the net position. The dethroned kings or queens retain the points they accumulated together and build on that total when they partner up again as kings or queens. Challengers do not keep the 3 points they win to dethrone the kings or queens. This new team starts with zero points and accumulates points together as the kings or queens. After the server feeds the ball, the point starts. The first team to 15 points wins.

167—SERVE AND VOLLEY-VOLLEY GAME

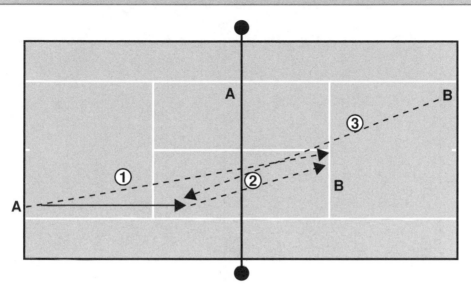

Objective
This game works on service placement, approach volleys, and finishing volleys.

Description
This game emphasizes serving down the center (T) of the service court, working on the approach, and finishing volleys during match play.

Execution
Team A and team B should position themselves in the standard doubles position. Only one serve is allowed in this game per team and per player. Team A serves the first ball down the center (T) of the deuce service court to team B and closes in to hit the approach volley back to the same place the server served it. The receiver on the deuce side of the court of team B must return the serve, trying to hit it low to the feet of team A's server. Team A's server, after hitting the approach volley back to the same place he or she hit the serve, should close in and try to hit a second volley winner. After this three-hit combination, play continues until one team wins the point. Each server serves 15-point games and then rotates.

Tip
When trying to hit an approach volley, players must stutter step or split step before hitting, hit the ball out in front, and move forward to the ball. They should not wait for the ball to come to them.

168—MEDUSA PASSING-SHOT GAME

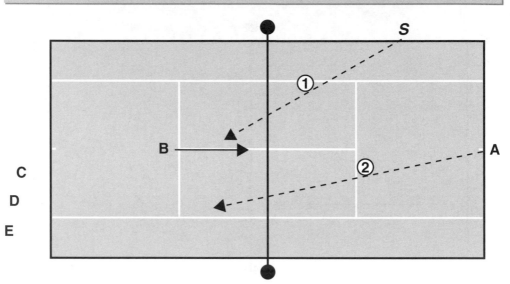

Objective

This game works on approach shots and passing shots.

Description

This is a great game to play with four or more players. Players attempt to win points by hitting passing shots against the player dubbed Medusa, queen of a million arms and hands, up at the net.

Execution

A server feeds balls from a position to the side and off the court. Challenging players B, C, D, and E line up at the center (T) behind the baseline. Player A is positioned behind the baseline on the opposite side of the court. The server feeds a ball into the midcourt section of the court to player B. Player B moves forward to hit an approach shot and then closes in on the net. Player A, Medusa, attempts to hit a passing shot past player B. Both players play out the point. When the point is over, player B returns to the end of the line, and it's player C's turn. Lobs are not allowed on the first passing shot. A challenger who wins three points becomes the passing-shot queen, Medusa.

Variation

With eight or more players, players should team up and play with same rules except that the doubles alleys are good.

Tip

One of the most important principles in the use of passing shots is keeping the ball low at the net player's feet. This action forces the volleyer to hit up, decreasing the opportunity to make an aggressive half volley or approach volley. Topspin balls drop faster than flat or underspin balls do, so players should try to use substantial topspin when hitting the blistering passing shot.

169—HALF-VOLLEY PASSING-SHOT CHALLENGE GAME

Objective

This challenge works players' half-volleying skills, passing shot, and point-finishing strategy.

Description

This game helps players develop the touch needed for half volleying.

Execution

Team A is three feet behind the service line. Team B is behind the opposite baseline. A server behind the net post on team A's side of the court starts the point by feeding a baseline shot to team B. Team B attempts to hit a passing shot, which they may not lob. Team A moves up to catch the shot as a half volley and then closes in to finish the point. After team A hits the half volley, both teams try to win the point. They play 21-point games and then rotate players.

Tip

Players having problems hitting half volleys may be trying to shovel the ball over the net with the hips above the ball. They should keep the hips and knees lower than the ball by using the thigh muscles to maintain a strong foundation. The hitting arm should be firm and the wrist and grip tight so that the head of the racket is solid as the player comes through the shot.

170—OVERHEAD SMASH GAME

Objective

This game emphasizes hitting the overhead to win the point.

Description

The drill helps players shorten their backswings so they can catch the ball farther in front, quicken their reaction time, quicken their footwork by emphasizing the ready hop, and work the point from a defensive position.

Execution

Two players, team A, are at the net, and two players, team B, are behind the opposite baseline. A server stands behind the players on the baseline and feeds a semidifficult overhead to team A. Team A attempts to hit and put away the overhead, which team B tries to retrieve. Team B then tries to hit passing shots or lobs to win the point. When a team loses a point, another team of players, team C or D, rotates in. The first team to 21 points wins.

Tip

Players should let the racket head lead as they would in serving and make sure that they get underneath the ball. The ball will bounce in front of them when they are in the correct position.

171—TEAM MERRY-GO-ROUND GAME

Objective

This game focuses on improving team communication, overheads, lobs, ground strokes, doubles strategy, and volley placement.

Description

Six or more players can play this action-packed game. Players learn how to identify and react to different shots, place shots, and hustle to cover and re-cover from hitting and winning points.

Execution

Team A, the kings or queens of the court, is in standard doubles formation on one side of the court. Challenging teams—B, C, and D—are on the opposite side, one behind another next to the doubles sideline and service line. A server stands to the side of the court on team A's (kings or queens) side. On the server's cue, the first challenging team, team B, sidesteps along the service line, sprints forward toward the net, taps it with their rackets, and shuffles backward in preparation for an overhead. The server feeds a deep lob over challenging team B. Team B must react, recover the lob, and play out the point. If team A wins the point, they remain the kings or queens and keep that point. If team B wins the point, team A runs to the end of the line of challenging teams. Team B has five seconds (counted down by the server) to run the net posts (team members run around opposite net posts to cover both sides) and get into standard doubles position before challenging team C completes the lob recovery. Teams play out the point. The first team to 21 wins the game.

Variation

The server can use overheads, dropshots, or a combination of shots instead of just lobs. Teams rotate only on their side of the court instead of running from one side to the other. If there are six or more teams involved, the merry-go-round game can be very exciting for all involved, because teams must really concentrate on hitting, moving, and placement of shots so as not to set up their teammate or the team moving in and playing just behind them to get crushed. Instructors or players can experiment with the original execution and use virtually any shot or combination of shots to keep the action exhilarating and educational.

Tip

Players should return a lob with a lob hit diagonally to use the additional five feet of extra court.

172—PEG-LEG DOUBLES GAME

Objective

This game emphasizes consistency and placement.

Description

Players use only half of the doubles court, playing out points and games cross-court. Players must work to keep the ball in play and away from the volleyer. Players must use all types of shots to keep the net player from stealing the ball out of the air.

Execution

Teams are positioned in standard doubles formation. Team A serves into the deuce court. Team B returns crosscourt. Teams play crosscourt only, including use of the doubles alley. Net players may try to poach once the serve is in play. Net players from both teams may only hit crosscourt shots, such as volleys, drop volleys, or overheads. Teams play an entire set, switching serves and positions after every game and using regular scoring.

Variation

The serving team uses the serve-and-volley tactic on every first serve. Alternatively, the serving team may be restricted to one serve per point per game.

Tip

Players having trouble stroking solid service returns should be sure that they aren't standing flat-footed, a stance that slows reaction to the ball. Players should keep their feet moving while the server is setting up, split step as the server strikes the ball, and move forward when stroking.

Movement and Conditioning

Tennis players need to be not only quick, agile, and smart, but also strong. Strength counts for 60 percent of tennis fitness makeup. Players who perform a comprehensive workout program will maximize their physical conditioning and stay at the top of their game. Working on improving strength, flexibility, and cardiovascular capacity by using on- and off-court training 12 months a year will also help players minimize pesky tennis injuries. The demands of playing tennis for fun or in tournaments can appear to be a continuous series of emergencies—sprinting to the ball, quickly changing direction, stretching, lunging, stopping, starting, on all types of surfaces and in all types of weather. Being able to perform these actions, while also maintaining proper balance and technique throughout a match, is critical for optimal performance on the court. Tennis takes years of practice, so players' bodies must be able to sustain the grueling hours, months, and years of training. Players should remember that the mind, body, and spirit are the greatest assets they have for any sport. They must keep them in shape!

chapter 15

Endurance Training

Nowadays most players use such tricky game plans that it will be a cold day in Hades before their opponents ever see a ball land anywhere close to them. All players must therefore have superb speed and court coverage. They must be able to last out points when the opponent has them running from corner to corner, up to the net, and then back behind the baseline for a topspin lob. And, oh yeah, they must be able to recover in 30 seconds to play the next point with as much intensity as they did the last. Agility and athletic proficiency are keys to playing hard and hitting shots, and they are crucial to all on-court movement, but speed is what will get players there. Therefore, players must embrace the hard work it takes to become tennis fit. Sprinting, changing direction quickly, reaching, stretching, lunging, stopping, bending, leaping, and making explosive starts and stops are all characteristics of the fitness demands of tennis today. By mixing in flexibility, strength, endurance, power, agility, speed, body composition, and aerobic and anaerobic fitness, players will improve their tennis games tremendously. This chapter is filled with wonderful on-court speed and agility drills. Players who practice them with discipline will reach their tennis fitness goals.

173—POINT AND GO

Objective

This drill teaches players the skills necessary for quick changes of direction.

Description

This drill helps players build the dexterity they need for changing direction quickly, sprinting forward, backpedaling, leaping, and lunging. The drill can have a player sprinting from side to side, up and back, or diagonally forward and backward.

Execution

Players spread out in the backcourt area and stand in the ready position facing the net. A leader, standing directly in front of the group, extends either arm and points to the side, forward, backward, or forward or backward at an angle. Players respond to the pointing movement by sprinting in the direction in which the leader points. The leader lets the players sprint a few steps and then points in another direction. He or she makes the players sprint in all directions, causing them to change direction quickly. Two- or three-minute periods of sprinting followed by 30-second rest periods is a good routine. The length and number of sprinting periods should increase as players build endurance.

174—DARK SHADOW

Objective

This drill develops quick reflexes, explosive starts, and sudden stops while executing tennis strokes.

Description

This drill is a fantastic way for players to learn how to move quickly to the ball and change direction with the explosive burst of speed needed to recover drop shots or return of serves.

Execution

Players pair off with each holding a racket in the hitting hand. One member of each pair is the leader; the other is the dark shadow. The leader assumes the ready position facing the net in the backcourt area. The shadow, also in the ready position, stands approximately three feet behind the leader. The leader then simulates a movement, any movement that players must make in actual tennis play. The leader can pivot and swing for a forehand and backhand or run forward to play a short ball either forehand or backhand. The shadow imitates the leader's movements. The drill continues with the leader trying to lose or confuse the shadow. After three or four minutes of action, players rest for 30 seconds. They reverse roles and resume the drill.

175—SHUTTLE RUN

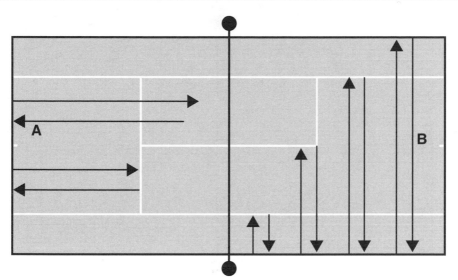

Objective

The purpose of this drill is to improve speed, endurance, quick changes of direction, and recovery, and build up the muscles in the hamstring and thigh area.

Description

This drill, often known as the suicide drill, is one of the most hated but simplest on-court exercises to improve overall speed and fitness on the court. In this drill, players can impart explosive starts and stops to the ball. Tennis isn't about long-distance running; players should train to be explosive and fast on the court.

Execution

Players (A) sprint from the baseline to the service line and back five times, trying to change direction quickly. They repeat the same routine from the baseline to the net.

Variation

Players (B) start on the outside doubles sideline, sprint to touch each line on the court with a racket in hand, and return to the doubles sideline. They do this three times in a row.

Tip

Anyone who plays tennis must be in good physical condition. Exercise is the key to success on the tennis court.

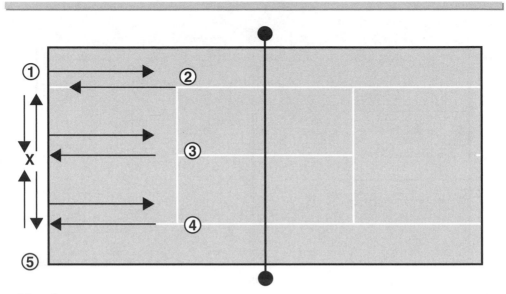

Objective

This drill helps to improve speed and quick change of direction. By moving in sequential patterns, players develop certain footwork so that it becomes second nature.

Description

This drill simulates the footwork and direction players will be moving to cover the backcourt area during match play. The drill also emphasizes the explosive, fast movements needed to hit certain shots on the court.

Execution

Players begin at position X, as shown in the diagram, holding a racket. They sprint to base 1, touch the junction between the baseline and sideline with one foot, and touch the ground in front of them with the racket. Players then return to position X. They repeat the movement to all the other bases (2, 3, 4, and 5), as shown in the diagram, except that they run backward to and from base 3. They repeat the sequence three times and time themselves. Players should try to beat their times in the next training session.

Tip

Players should never start a sprinting drill with cold muscles. To warm up, players should jog around the tennis court six times—first lap forward, second lap sidestepping facing the court, third lap reverse sidestepping by turning away from the court, fourth lap backpedaling, fifth lap sprinting, and the sixth lap walking it off. They can use this warm-up routine before conditioning drills or hitting drills.

177—COURT CIRCUIT

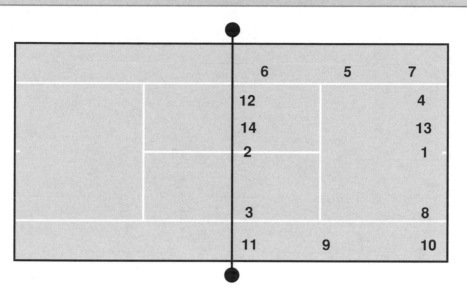

Objective
This drill improves speed, stamina, and proficiency on the court.

Description
This drill helps build footwork, speed, agility, and dexterity for hitting and recovering easy and hard-to-reach shots during competition. The drill helps players become comfortable with all areas of the court and be aware of where they are on the court during heated competition.

Execution
The diagram shows where to set up flat sprinting markers. Players follow the route from 1 to 14, sprinting as fast as they can. They run backward from 5 to 6, 4 to 7, 9 to 10, and 12 to 13. They touch the ground with a hand at each point, and at the front of the court they touch the net.

Variation
Players can leap up and over cones placed on the designated stop points.

Tip
Some players may feel like they have the speed of Superman, the agility and dexterity of Spider-Man, and the gracefulness of a prima ballerina, but still can't figure out how to run down certain shots. These players are prime candidates for spending more time working their on-court footwork. Players should practice any kind of fancy, speedy footwork routine possible and watch the level of their on-court readiness soar!

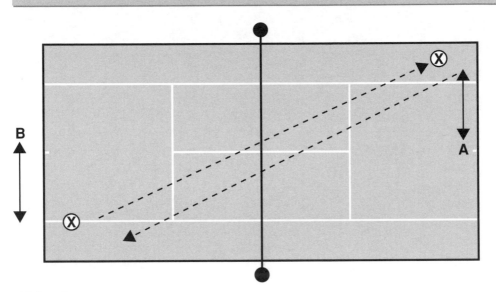

Objective

This way of drilling keeps stamina training interesting because players are hitting a tennis ball at the same time.

Description

This drill allows players to train on court for superior court stamina and at the same time practice tennis by working on consistency, direction, and control.

Execution

Players A and B rally crosscourt to each other trying to hit a specific target (X) placed in the corner where the doubles alley and baseline meet. After each shot, players return to the center (T), hitting ground strokes on the run. They perform this drill for five minutes, change sides of the court, and repeat. If they can maintain a continuous rally and push hard to return to the center (T) after each shot, they will find this a top conditioning drill and lots of fun as well.

Variation

Players can hit down-the-line forehands and backhands, or any combination of shots, such as two forehands crosscourt then one backhand crosscourt.

Tip

Tennis players need to be in top physical condition to keep the progression process flowing smoothly. Conditioning drills combined with hitting balls creates a "light at the end of the tunnel" effect for many players who hate just drilling or working out to stay in tennis shape.

179—RUN, HIT, AND RECOVER

Objective
This drill improves court movement and builds leg strength.

Description
Not only do players need to be quick in moving along the baseline, they also need to be agile enough to move explosively to short balls, sharp-angled shots, and drop shots.

Execution
Player A stands on the baseline, and player B is up at net. Player B, armed with a basket of balls, alternately feeds player A short balls, drop shots, sharp-angled balls, and deep ground strokes. Player A's goal is to hit every ball and return it crosscourt deep without missing. Players should try this drill with 20 balls and work up to 100.

Variation
To improve their weak shots, players can hit balls to any area on the court.

180—STEP-OUT VOLLEY

Objective
This drill helps develop the footwork technique and agility needed to hit volleys or ground strokes using the open stance.

Description
The step-out technique facilitates preparation for using the open stance and recovering quickly.

Execution
Players position themselves around the court facing the net, each with enough room to move five to six feet in all directions. On a leader's cue, players step out to the side with the left foot. The hips should face the net. Players do not close the hips with a crossover first step. Together, players perform a split step, step out with the left foot, and then perform a crossover movement into the ball, keeping the back knee bent low to the ground to simulate proper volley footwork. They then split step to recovery. Players perform this movement 20 times without the racket for the forehand volley and 20 times for the backhand volley, all at maximum speed. They repeat the drill with the racket in hand, resting for one minute after each set.

Tip
Players must be sure to maintain correct posture while performing the drill. Good posture helps players develop strong, sound volleys.

181—QUICK-FEET ALLEY

Objective

This drill improves the agility and speed needed for good court movement.

Description

Players use the alley to quicken and tighten the compact movement needed for strong, controlled volleys.

Execution

Players position themselves one behind another in one of the doubles alleys, four or five feet apart. Players should be in the standard ready position without rackets. On a leader's cue, players explode into quick running-in-place steps for 15 seconds. On the second cue, players split step, step out with the left foot, crossover step with the right foot, keep the back knee low for a low volley, and hold for 10 seconds. On the third cue, players recover with a split step. On the fourth cue, players run in place for 15 seconds. They repeat the cycle for the backhand low volley, rest for one minute, and repeat the cycle for the high forehand volley and high backhand volley. They rest for one minute and repeat the cycle for the waist-high volley. They do the complete cycle two or three times.

182—DEXTERITY BALL

Objective

This drill teaches better movement to the ball, develops agility, and quickens reflexes.

Description

Two or more players can perform this drill. The players do not have rackets.

Execution

Players pair up. Player A holds two balls and takes the leader position. Player B performs the catching and rolling action. Player A kneels approximately four feet in front of player B. Player B stands in the standard ready position in front of player A. Player A starts the drill by rolling one ball wide to player B's forehand side. Player B split steps and performs the stepping-out footwork, recovers the ball, and rolls it back quickly to player A's hands. Player A rolls the second ball wide to player B's backhand side. Player B split steps, performs the stepping-out footwork, recovers the ball, and rolls it back quickly to player A's hands. Players should perform this drill at maximum speed for two minutes and then switch positions. Players work up to doing five solid sets in each position.

183—SKIING FOR SKILL

Objective

This drill improves balance and lateral movement on court.

Description

Starting behind the doubles alley and balancing a ball on the strings of a racket, players weave through markers set out along the baseline, racing against time.

Execution

Six or more flat markers or cones should be placed three feet apart along the length of the baseline. Players stand off the court behind one of the side alleys. On cue, the first player steps up to the first marker, balancing a ball on the racket strings. The goal is to shuffle laterally, weaving through markers without dropping the ball off the racket, to the end of the baseline and back in 20 seconds. Players who drop the ball start over from the beginning. Players should keep trying until they successfully complete the drill within 20 seconds. Player can try three times to complete the drill.

Variation

Players can bounce the ball down or up or do a combination of both.

Tip

The center of gravity, the point at which the body balances perfectly, is the key to staying in the action. Players should keep their eyes focused on the ball while maintaining control of their center of gravity.

chapter 16

In-Season Maintenance

Most athletes who compete in tennis realize that to perform at peak levels on the court they must follow an on- and off-court physical conditioning program. Players who work to improve their fitness through extra training other than hitting tennis balls are more likely to succeed in long, grueling matches. Physical training greatly improves performance on the court. An athlete who prepares physically for a match will also be prepared mentally.

Extra off-court training for upcoming matches gives players confidence that they are fully prepared and ready to play. This confidence enables players to perform during the match without pressing, rushing, or choking during heated competition. To win consistently, competitors must combine speed, quickness, and stamina into their physical conditioning. To improve their play, players need to be in the best cardiovascular shape possible. They can do that only by adding conditioning activities to their training schedules. Almost any aerobic activity will increase cardiovascular endurance, but players must regulate the duration, frequency, and intensity of workouts to optimize their fitness for tennis. Tennis players do not have to spend hours on the treadmill or in the pool to reach their physical peak. Endurance training for tennis requires enough aerobic conditioning to see players through three sets; 20 to 30 minutes three times a week is usually sufficient.

Players looking to shed a few pounds should increase their aerobic activity. Otherwise, they'll be lugging dead weight around the court. Spending time in the gym will help build supple, lean muscles that will help power players' strokes through to the end of a three-hour, three-set tennis match. Good muscle tone helps protect the joints, tendons, and ligaments from the constant shock they take during a match. The successful transfer of force from the lower body to the upper body generates most of the power in a tennis stroke. Because shots will only be as strong as the weakest link in this chain of power, players must develop all of the major muscle groups: legs, abs, back, chest, shoulders, and arms.

A specific, comprehensive physical conditioning program will improve players' confidence, improve their technique and power, reduce the number and severity of tennis-related injuries, delay fatigue, promote faster recovery after competition, reduce the number of down hours after training, and enable the development of better athletes. The exercises in this section provide an on- and off-court training program for total-body conditioning of tennis players.

184—DEEP-CHAIR PUSH-UPS

Objective

The purpose of this exercise is to increase the range of motion of all joints in the body.

Description

A good basic stretching program keeps limbs and joints functioning through a full range of motion. Benefits of stretching include reduction of muscle tension and correction of postural imbalances that often develop in tennis, which stresses the joints and muscles unequally on opposite sides of the body.

Execution

Men and women perform different versions of deep-chair aided push-ups. Men place their feet on a chair placed behind them and place each hand on a chair positioned beside them. They do regular push-ups, lowering the chest close to the ground between the two chairs. Women use the same method except that they keep the feet on the ground instead of using a chair positioned behind them. Players try to do three sets of 12, resting 45 seconds between sets.

Tip

Players should warm up their muscles with a low-intensity activity like jumping jacks or jogging in place. They stretch to a point that's challenging but not painful and hold for 15 to 20 seconds, breathing normally. They repeat each stretch two to three times on both sides of the body.

185—CALF STRETCH

Objective

The purpose of this exercise is to stretch the calf muscle, Achilles tendon, and lower hamstrings.

Description

The calf muscle is the fleshy, muscular back part of the leg between the knee and ankle.

Execution

Players stand in front of a wall or pole with one foot two or three feet behind the other and the toes pointed forward. Keeping the back knee straight and heels on the floor, players bend the front knee and lean forward until they feel the stretch. After 30 seconds they switch legs and repeat. Next, they stand erect with feet together and both heels on the ground. They lean forward until they feel tightness in the calves and Achilles tendons. After holding the position for 30 seconds, they release the stretch and return to standing position.

186—HAMSTRING STRETCH

Objective
This exercise stretches the hamstring, lower-back muscles, and upper-calf muscle.

Description
The stretch focuses on two tendons at the rear hollow of the knee.

Execution
From a seated position, players bend the left knee and place the sole of the left foot against the inside of the right knee. Keeping the back and right knee as straight as possible, they reach toward the foot with both hands. They hold each stretch for 30 seconds, switch legs, and repeat.

Variations
For the standing hamstring stretch, players stand in an upright position with knees locked. They bend forward slowly, moving the hands down the back of the legs toward the ankles until they feel tightness in the hamstrings. For the hurdler's hamstring stretch, players sit on the floor with one leg turned backward and the other extended forward (high hurdler's position). They bend the torso and head down toward the knee until they feel tightness. Players hold each position for 30 seconds and then relax and return to the original position.

187—POSTERIOR SHOULDER STRETCH

Objective
The purpose of this exercise is to stretch the shoulder rotators and upper-back (scapular) muscles.

Description
The shoulder is the part of the body between the neck and upper arm or forelimb. The scapular is the area of the back that lies between the shoulders.

Execution
Players stand and hold the left arm out in front. They place the right hand behind the left elbow and pull the elbow across the body with the right hand. They let the left hand fall over the shoulder, but they don't let the trunk rotate. They hold for 30 seconds, switch arms, and repeat.

Tip
Players should never stretch a muscle during any exercise to the level of discomfort or pain or they run the risk of tearing it.

188—STORK QUADRICEPS STRETCH

Objective

This exercise stretches the quadriceps and shin muscles.

Description

The quadriceps are located in the thigh.

Execution

Players stand on one leg and grasp the other foot or ankle. Keeping the back straight, they pull the foot up behind the buttocks so that the knee points to the ground (without twisting the knee). For balance, they extend the arm in front of them or hold onto a wall. They hold for 30 seconds, switch legs, and repeat.

Variations

For the hurdler's quadriceps stretch, players lie on their back with both legs together. They grasp the left ankle with the left hand, slowly pull the ankle toward the waist, and lower the head toward the floor until they feel tightness in the quadriceps. For the prone quadriceps stretch, players lie on the stomach with both legs stretched out behind them. They bend the left knee toward the buttocks, grasp the foot with the left hand, and pull it directly toward the buttocks. They hold for 30 seconds, relax, and repeat using the right leg.

Tip

Players must be patient, work within their limits, and stay relaxed.

189—LEG EXTENSION

Objective

The leg extension targets the quadriceps; it's also good for knee-injury prevention and rehabilitation.

Description

Players extend the legs upward against the resistance of added weight, straightening the knees fully but not hyperextending them. They slowly lower the weight to the starting position.

Execution

When sitting in the leg extension machine, players should adjust the backrest so that the knees bend at the edge of the seat. The lower pad should be just above the ankles. Players put the feet behind the pad and lift until both legs are almost fully extended. They pause, slowly lower the feet to the starting position, switch legs, and repeat.

190—LEG CURL

Objective
The leg curl works the often ignored hamstrings, which are key muscles for sprinting, backpedaling, and stability when playing low balls.

Description
Players should slowly curl the feet toward the buttocks and then slowly return the weight to the starting position. The knees should never hyperextend when performing this exercise.

Execution
Players lie face down on the curl machine, letting the leg pads touch just above the ankles. Starting with the knees bent slightly, players slowly bring both feet up toward the buttocks, trying to achieve at least a 90-degree angle. They hold this position for a moment and then slowly let the weight down.

191—LEG PRESS

Objective
This multiple-joint training exercise works the buttocks, quadriceps, hamstrings, and calves.

Description
The leg press is great for developing overall leg strength, which helps build stamina and stopping and starting ability.

Execution
Players position themselves in the leg-press machine with the back flat against the backrest and the feet on the platform shoulder-width apart. They bend the legs at a 90-degree angle and slowly push the feet against the platform until the legs are extended. They hold for a moment and then slowly return to the starting position. To target the inner and outer thigh muscles and the gluteus (used for side shuffling, up-and-back movements, low-ball hitting stances, and open-stance strokes), they place the feet farther apart with the toes pointing outward.

Tip
Explosive starts, stops, leaping, lunging, bending, or sprinting can't happen without the strength of the lower body. Even to be able to execute fundamental ground strokes, players must be physically able to move out of the ready position.

192—COMPOUND ROW

Objective
This exercise develops the rhomboids, trapezius, posterior deltoid, and biceps.

Description
Rowing is a great back developer and is useful for the prevention of injury and rehabilitation of the rotator cuff. Rowing also builds power on the backhand, especially for hitting high balls with the one-handed stroke.

Execution
Players sit with the back straight, feet braced against the crossbar, and legs slightly bent. With a neutral grip (palms facing each other), they pull their arms toward them and then slowly extend their arms to a straight position. The elbows should be close to the body and near the waistline.

193—LATERAL PULLDOWN

Objective
This exercise develops the latissimus dorsi and bicep muscles, which help absorb shock during forward arm movements.

Description
This all-purpose back exercise targets the lats, or latissimus, the muscles used for the serve and overhead smash.

Execution
Players sit facing the machine with the feet flat on the floor. They grasp the bar with the hands shoulder-width apart and palms toward them. They pull down slowly to the upper chest, keeping the head and back straight and the elbows close to the sides. The release should be slow to prevent the machine from overstretching the shoulders. The rotator cuff muscles can be strained if the grip is wider than shoulder-width or if the exercise is performed by lowering the bar behind the neck.

Tip
Players must know that it takes more than a killer desire to nail a service ace or a blistering overhead smash. It takes many hours of training and building the muscles associated with hitting serves and overheads. Learning how to properly train the lats will increase service and overhead strength and will help keep players free of shoulder injuries.

194—OVERHEAD PRESS

Objective
This exercise works the front and sides of the shoulders.

Description
This is a general upper-body conditioning and strengthening exercise.

Execution
Players should adjust the seat height so that the handles are about even with the shoulders. They sit in the machine and hold the handles with the palms facing up. They slowly push the arms up to full extension but don't lock them. After holding for two to three seconds, they slowly bring the weight down.

Variation
For push-ups from the floor, players place the hands shoulder-width apart with the body in a straight line from the toes to the head. They slowly lower themselves until the upper arm is parallel to the ground. They push themselves upward until the elbows are completely straight, and they round the back outward as a cat would. This rounding motion at the end of the push-up is significant and increases the work done by the muscles that stabilize the shoulder blade.

195—CHEST PRESS

Objective
This exercise develops the pectoralis major and minor, serratus anterior, triceps, and anterior deltoid.

Description
This movement primarily targets the chest muscles but also works the front shoulders and triceps.

Execution
Players sit with the feet flat on the floor and the hands shoulder-width apart on the handles. Keeping the back straight against the backrest, they push out from the chest until both arms are fully extended but not locked. They hold for two seconds and then return to the starting position.

Tip
Players should remember to warm up before performing any muscle-strengthening or muscle-endurance program. Players should exhale during the pressing part of the routine and inhale as they return the weight to its starting or resting position. Players should get into the good habit of breathing, as it can be too easy to hold their breath while weight lifting.

196—LATERAL DELTOID RAISE

Objective
This exercise develops the sides of the shoulder used for hitting strong one-handed backhands.

Description
This exercise targets the usually underdeveloped sides of the shoulder muscles. Development of these muscles is vital in protecting the rotator cuff and strengthens the backhand, especially the one-handed topspin backhand.

Execution
Players sit with the back straight and the chest up. The roller pads should rest just above the elbows. Players grip the handles loosely and slowly push up with the elbows until the arms are at a 90-degree angle to the body. They hold for a second and then slowly return the elbows to the side.

197—TORSO ROTATION

Objective
This exercise strengthens the internal and external obliques, the body's core.

Description
This excellent exercise develops the rotational strength required on ground strokes and serves, and helps protect the lower back from the twisting and turning movements that are essential in tennis.

Execution
Players hold a bar behind the neck with both hands, keeping the back straight and the hips facing forward. Keeping the rest of the body steady, they twist from the waist, first to the right and then to the left, as far as they can.

Variation
To improve specific strengths needed for tennis, players can try trunk twists using a medicine ball.

Tip
By strengthening the internal and external obliques, players are strengthening the body's core. The core is the power transfer station, which includes the abs, lower and upper back, and sides. Players who work to strengthen these muscles will notice increased power when hitting using the open stance on ground strokes and swinging volleys.

198—SPINAL TWIST

Objective
This exercise stretches the lower back, buttocks, and upper-shoulder muscle.

Description
The lower back is the region of the vertebrae nearest the lower end of the spine.

Execution
From a seated position, players bend the right leg and place the right ankle on the outside of the left knee. They take the left arm over the right knee and while looking over the right shoulder, they slowly turn the shoulders and torso to the right. They hold for 30 seconds, switch legs, and repeat.

Variation
For the knees-to-chest stretch, players lie flat on the ground with the legs stretched out in front of them. They bring the knees together toward the chest by grasping the lower legs just below the knees and guiding them up and flat against the chest. After holding for 30 seconds, they relax and straighten out the legs. They perform at least three sets of 30-second holds.

199—CRUNCHES

Objective
Crunches strengthen the abdominal muscles that protect the lower back and add power to all strokes.

Description
This exercise helps to develop a strong rectus abdominis (trunk), which is the source of many movements in tennis and allows the upper body to stay synchronized with the lower body.

Execution
Players lie on their back with knees bent, feet flat on the floor, and hands behind the head. As they slowly lift the head and shoulders toward the knees, they contract the stomach muscles, breathing out as they rise up and in as they go down. The head should be in line with the neck, and the eyes should focus on the ceiling. They hold for a five-second count and then slowly lower themselves to the floor.

200—SPEEDY INTERVAL TRAINING

Objective
This workout improves heart-rate recovery time and raises the anaerobic threshold.

Description
By incorporating intervals (periodic bursts of speed followed by resting cycles) into an off-court training program, players accomplish two things. First, they improve their heart-rate recovery time so that they won't be gasping for air after a long rally. Second, they raise their anaerobic threshold (the point at which the muscles go into oxygen debt and become exhausted) so that they stay fresher longer.

Execution
Players should find a track or smooth straightaway for their training. They sprint 60 meters 10 or 12 times with a rest of one and a half or two minutes after each sprint. Then they sprint 100 meters 8 or 10 times with a rest of two or two and half minutes after each sprint. They sprint 200 meters 10 or 12 times with a six- to eight- minute rest after each sprint. Finally, they sprint 400 meters four to six times with a five- or seven-minute rest after each sprint.

201—BASIC INTERVAL TRAINING

Objective
This workout develops capacity for high-intensity sessions with adequate rest intervals.

Description
Players rated at 2.5 and above probably find themselves rushing the net one minute and rallying along the baseline the next. Their interval training should follow a similar mix-and-match approach. Varying the length and intensity of each cycle will mimic their on-court actions and challenge their muscles.

Execution
- Sprint for 10 seconds and walk for 5.
- Sprint for 15 seconds and walk for 10.
- Sprint for 30 seconds and walk for 15.
- Sprint for 5 seconds and walk for 5.

Variation
Players can continue to mix up the length of the sprints and recovery periods, but no sprint should last longer than 90 seconds.

Tip
To improve explosive speed on the court, players can also try running up stairs or spinning.

202—CROSS-TRAINING

Objective
Cross-training adds variety to keep players fresh and on top of their fitness development.

Description
Developing an effective cross-training program is as simple as swapping the stair climber for the treadmill or taking a step-aerobics class. Players should remember that they need activities that involve the energy systems and movement patterns of tennis. Repeating the same cardiovascular activities gets the body in a rut and lowers benefits, so mixing it up is key (hence the name "cross-training").

Execution
The following is a suggested cross-training schedule:

Monday, Wednesday, Friday
1. Weight training
2. Cardiovascular training in spinning classes, on a ski machine, an elliptical trainer or other such machine or class

Tuesday, Thursday
1. Track training using the basic or speedy interval training schedule
   - Sprint for 10 seconds and walk for 5.
   - Sprint for 15 seconds and walk for 10.
   - Sprint for 30 seconds and walk for 15.
   - Sprint for 45 seconds and walk for 20.
   - Jump rope in two-minute intervals for 10 sets.

Variation
To improve coordination and balance, players can try yoga, pilates, or kick boxing. These disciplines help keep stress levels under control, build total body strength, increase balance, and loosen up the body so that players can put more power behind each shot.

Tip
Players should warm up with a light three- to five-minute jog to prepare the muscles for exercise. Players should know that tennis isn't solely aerobic; in fact, it's primarily anaerobic. So incorporating aerobic exercise such as jogging, spinning, and swimming combined with anaerobic exercise such as interval training that includes short bursts of sprinting speed helps players of any level reach the optimal physical condition needed to play good tennis.

203—SURFACE CROSS-TRAINING

Objective
This cross-training program is favorable to playing on different court surfaces, such as clay, hard, and grass.

Description
Pros who compete on a variety of surfaces often change the length of intervals based on the type of court they're competing on.

Execution
Playing on clay usually means playing longer points, so players training to play on a surface like that at the French Open should train at longer intervals. For training to play on a surface like Wimbledon's or on any fast indoor surface, the intervals should be shorter. Those who play most of their matches on clay or other slow surfaces should concentrate on 200- to 400-meter sprints with a one- to two-minute rest between sprints. For hard-court and grass play, they should incorporate shorter intervals of 50 to 100 meters with a 30- to 60-second breather after each set.

Tip
The most important aspect of any cross-training program is rest for the mind.

Competitive Group Games

Teaching game-based versus skill-based lessons is the unique formula that's keeping tennis alive and thriving today. In a nutshell, game-based teaching simply means instructing with gamelike situations that approach the authenticity of actual match-play competition. Participating in group lessons is a wonderful way for players to learn the fundamentals and practice what they've learned while having a lot of fun at the same time. Instructors understand that giving effective lessons to a group of children or adults is a constant challenge to their teaching ability. In teaching the fundamentals of the game, they must deal with individuals of varying age, physical ability, learning skills, athletic background, and personality. Instructors have to work harder when giving group lessons, especially if their aim is to give some undivided attention to each student. They have to keep the balls coming to the players, keep them moving so that boredom won't set in, and keep the lessons interesting, educational, and enjoyable while providing a stream of encouragement and advice.

The answer is balance. Balance between the two teaching styles for teaching group lessons to children or adults is essential to keeping students wanting to play and learn. Instructors should remember that tennis is a game first and should be fun, but that offering a dollop of learning opportunities must be part of the equation. As an instructor, I have experienced many teaching challenges throughout my years. Two experiences have helped me through the tough times of teaching. First was tasting the sweet juice of a freshly sliced pineapple while sunning in Ocho Rios, Jamaica. Second was watching students with whom I've worked, cried, and laughed come back after graduating from grammar school, high school, or college to tell me how much they miss me and how much they loved my classes. I still can't figure out which is sweeter.

This part of *The Tennis Drill Book* delves into games for children and adults that reinforce the drills that players have worked on in the other parts. Whether players prefer to enjoy tennis games in a structured class or with a group of players practicing against the backboard, they will find plenty of exciting ways to keep their game a-grooving.

chapter 17

Teaching Group Games

Most people learn tennis through group or multiplayer lessons. A well-organized group lesson keeps all players busy, learning, and having loads of fun. Children age 4 through 11 learn the fundamentals of playing tennis through game-based tactics that reinforce tennis techniques such as ground stroking, moving to the ball, hitting the ball, keeping score, and developing a mature approach to competition. Through game-based tactics, adults and juniors ages 12 and older develop not only the fundamentals of the game but also the physical and emotional maturity required of athletes.

A unique formula for teaching group lessons to juniors age 12 through 17 and adults of all levels is known as the five paradoxes of teaching group tennis. The first is self-esteem building versus critical thinking. By building students' self-esteem, instructors keep them coming back for more. Second is creating a fun environment versus a learning environment. Although drilling is necessary to developing tennis players of any age or level, with children it can be challenging, to say the least, for both instructors and young players. Children can't understand nor do they want to hear a bunch of technical mumbo jumbo. They just want to hit the ball, run after the ball, throw the ball, and kick the ball. The remedy is teaching with game-playing methods. This method feeds the energy and blossoming imaginations of eager young players. The balance between the two teaching styles is essential. Third is teaching game-based versus skill-based lessons. A real match environment during practice for junior and adult players will automatically improve their real match performance. Fourth is guided discovery versus command style, and fifth is student teaching and high retention versus verbal instructions and retention. Instructors who combine all five teaching styles into their teaching methods create the best learning environment for their students.

Adapted, by permission, from J. Dinoffer, 2002, "The five paradoxes of teaching group tennis to children," *ADDvantage Magazine* © USPTA pp. 12-14.

With the aid of entertaining and exciting tennis-related games collected in this chapter, parents and professional instructors can introduce a new and exciting way to teach tennis to children, juniors, and adults. In a nutshell, games are used primarily to teach developing players in an enjoyable way how to become mature physically and emotionally as skilled competitive tennis players. What better way to educate the mind, body, and spirit than through fun and games? Students will never forget the instructor or what they have learned and the fun they had while doing it. The pages to follow contain a plethora of activities, games, and instructional tips to keep all players, young or older, interested, excited, and enthusiastic, and keep lesson plans and instructors' imaginations fresh.

204—BALL PICKUP GAME

Objective

This game creates an interesting and enjoyable way for young children to clear balls from the court.

Description

Clearing balls from the court and returning them to the teaching cart is never the highlight of a student's tennis lesson. If this boring task can be made into a challenging, entertaining game, the students will find it enjoyable and will request to do it.

Execution

Instructors ask players to build a castle, teepee, or pyramid when they stack the balls on top of their rackets. Or they can ask players to make a pizza with the balls. Before the students put the pizza into the oven (ball cart), they tell the instructor what kind of pizza it is.

Tip

Instructors should always reward ball pickup. For example, the student who picks up the most balls gets to choose which game will be played.

205—ME AND MY SHADOW GAME

Objective

This game develops hand-eye coordination, footwork, and the ability to follow direction.

Description

This game helps young players use their imagination and choose the type of stroke they want to hit. It also keeps the other students involved while one student is hitting.

Execution

To ensure safety, students should be in a single-file line, not too close to each other. Poly spots (flat-colored place mats) can designate where students will stand so that they won't run into each other with their rackets. The first student in line hits a series of shots—forehands, backhands, volleys, and so on—and the other students pretend to be his or her shadow. The students mimic every movement, that is, the strokes and footwork.

206—OOPS! I FORGOT MY RACKET GAME

Objective

This game develops hand-eye coordination, ball tracking, ball sense, and gross motor ability.

Description

Before young players or even beginning players can master hitting a small tennis ball, the instructor should help them become familiar with the feel and dexterity of catching and throwing the ball.

Execution

Students are positioned three feet away from the tennis net. The instructor stands across the net opposite the students and tosses balls to them. Students must catch the ball on the first bounce and then toss it back over the net to the instructor or into a bucket. The instructor can vary the difficulty of the tosses.

Tip

The instructor should establish a reward system on the first day of lessons to motivate young players to follow directions, focus, and give their best when participating.

207—THROUGH THE TARGET GAME

Objective

This game develops hand-eye coordination, dexterity, gross motor skills, and athletic agility.

Description

This game helps players learn how to direct tennis balls to specific targets.

Execution

The instructor should position the players across the service line, standing next to each other. Cones, buckets, or tennis rackets standing butt down should be placed on the opposite side of the tennis net. Players enjoy throwing or hitting balls at targets. When a player hits a target, he or she earns a reward. The first player to hit a target gets to pick the next game for the day. This approach saves on ball pickup time!

Tip

This little game is a great way to teach young players how to score in tennis. For every target hit, that player should yell out a score, such as "Fifteen!" or "Thirty!" until four targets are hit. Then the player would yell "Game!" Six games wins the set, 12 wins the match.

208—POP-UP VOLLEY GAME

Objective

This game develops confidence up at the net, hand-eye coordination, fast reaction to the ball, and ball-tracking skills.

Description

This interesting twist on volleying helps young players develop a sense of volley eagerness. It makes them really hungry to "bop" or block the ball. Creating a fun environment for volleying also keeps young players from shying away from the net.

Execution

Players take positions lengthwise approximately three feet from the net. Players should be in squatting positions with rackets in hand and up in the volley position. The instructor stands on the other side of the net and tosses balls one at a time to the players. On cue from the instructor, the players pop up, hit a volley, and then squat again like jacks-in-the-box. If the player hits the volley, he or she gets to stand up and hit the next volley. If the player hits this volley, he or she may try to hit an overhead. If the player misses any one of the shots, he or she starts over from the squatting position. All players who successfully hit all three shots over the net win.

Variation

The instructor can turn this game into storybook volley land by assigning the name of a character to each student. On hearing his or her character mentioned in the story, the student pops up and hits a volley. For example, the frog (the player with the frog character pops up to hit a volley) telephones the turtle (the turtle pops up to hit a volley) and asks if the turtle wants to come over and share some pizza with rabbit (the rabbit pops up to hit a volley), and so on. Letting children choose their characters keeps them interested and can result in an interesting story line. The first few times you try this drill, you may want to come up with a few rounds so you're not left with pauses in the middle of the game while you try to think of what to say next.

Tip

If an oncoming tennis ball has ever hit you in the face or neck or even the back of your head while attempting to volley, then you realize how scary it can be. Multiply those feelings by a factor of ten, and you will understand why children and some adults are reluctant to jump into the volleying frying pan. Don't rush children or timid adults into volleying; let them show you by their willingness, excitement, and eagerness to "bop" the ball.

209—TIGER WOODS TENNIS GAME

Objective
This game develops racket and ball control.

Description
Players use some of the techniques of golf to aim the ball into the net as if they are putting the ball. They follow it up by hitting a serve toward a target. This game takes the pressure out of learning how to serve over the net, a difficult task for players who are only three feet tall.

Execution
Players form two lines behind the baseline or service line, depending on ability. A target and stack of balls on a racket are placed in front of each team. The first two players run forward and place a ball on top of a cone with the top cut off. Players hit the ball with their rackets using a golf swing (forehand) into the net. They retrieve the ball and serve it toward a target on the other side of the net. Players run back to their teams and tag the next player. The first team to hit the target or hit all balls over the net wins.

Variation
Players can use their backhand or their nondominant hand.

210—TENNIS FOR TOTS GAME

Objective
This game develops hand-eye coordination, balance, and ball sense.

Description
When tossing involves a bounce, it is best to match the word with the action. This exercise could involve the vocalization of three words (toss, bounce, and catch). Teaching a child to balance a ball on the racket demands body coordination and balance, and ups and downs are excellent for developing hand-eye coordination. Ups consist of bouncing the ball in the air with the racket. Downs involve consecutive bounces and hits off the court. A self-drop hit calls for the ball to be dropped close enough to the body to be hit after one bounce.

Execution
Players take positions across the baseline with rackets and balls. On the instructor's cue, each player places a ball on the strings of the racket and tries to balance the ball for 10 to 15 seconds without dropping it. Next, players try to hit as many ups as they can in 15 or 20 seconds without letting the ball drop. Next, players try to hit as many downs as they can in 15 or 20 seconds without losing control of the ball. Last, players try a combination of ups and downs.

Variation
Players can walk, run, skip, hop, or spin around during the game.

211—DUCK, DUCK, GOOSE TENNIS GAME

Objective

This game develops footwork, fast reaction to the ball, speed, athletic agility, and ball control.

Description

This game really gets players to concentrate on keeping the ball in play. If a player misses a shot into the net or hits it out of the court, then he or she must rely on speed and agility to outrun the other players trying to hit three consecutive balls over and in play before the player makes it back to home base. All players must focus.

Execution

Players position themselves in a single-file line behind the baseline or service line. The instructor feeds a ball to the first player in line, requiring the player to hit either forehand or backhand. If a player hits the ball over the net and in play, the instructor says, "Duck," and the player runs to the end of the line and is considered safe. If the player misses the shot, the instructor yells, "Goose!" and the player must run completely around the markers set up on the opposite side of the court and get back to the end of the line before the student standing in line hits two shots in a row over the net and in play. If the goose makes it back to home base in time, he or she doesn't receive a goose egg. But the goose who doesn't make it back in time receives a goose egg. Play a certain number of minutes or rounds, or until players start to lose focus. The player with the fewest goose eggs at the end of the game wins. Try not to make the focus of the game on scoring though. Encourage players to do their best each time it's their turn, regardless of the number of goose eggs he or she may have.

Variations

Players can use ground strokes, volleys, and overheads. The rules of the game can also be slightly adjusted. For example, line students one behind the other behind the center (T) of the service line or baseline. The instructor starts by feeding one ball to the first player in line. If the player hits the shot over the net and onto the court, the player is safe and can proceed to the end of the line. If the player misses the shot after two attempts, the instructor yells "Goose!" The player, with racket in hand, must spring from his side of the court, around the markers on the opposite side of the court, and back to the end of the line on his original side of the net before each student standing in line hits three balls in a row each over the net. If the runner (goose) makes it back before each student accomplishes this task, the goose doesn't receive a goose egg. If not, the player receives one goose egg.

212—TOTALLY TOUGH TENNIS GAME

Objective

This drill develops footwork, fast reaction to the ball, quick reflexes, evasive action to move away from the ball, speed, agility, and rapid change of direction.

Description

This game introduces the skill needed to keep the ball in play on the court. Players learn how to move, hit, and direct the ball to different areas of the court.

Execution

Players form two teams in front of a wall with rackets in hand. Each team has one ball. On cue, the first player in each line drop hits the ball against the wall. The next player in line moves forward and hits the ball and so on until someone misses. Rotation is continuous.

Variation

Teams can try to hit as many shots as possible in a timed session, use only the hands or feet, or use volleys or overheads.

213—AROUND THE TENNIS WORLD GAME

Objective

This game teaches players how to watch the ball, how to position themselves on the court, how to cover the court, and how the tennis scoring system works.

Description

This game encourages players to keep the ball in play, direct the ball to areas that will cause the opposing team to miss, and work together as a team.

Execution

The instructor forms two teams and positions players behind the service line facing each other. They use only the service-court area. Players hit the ball over the net into the opposite service court and go to the end of the line. The next player moves forward to play the return in a continuous hitting sequence. Teams score when opponents fail to return the ball. The first team to reach 10 wins.

Variation

Players attempt to hit 26 shots in succession (A through Z). With chalk, the instructor marks letters A to Z around the court, progressing from easy to difficult areas. Players are behind the baseline center (T). Players start at A and progress to the next letter by using designated strokes. Players who miss stay at that letter until they execute the stroke. The first player to Z wins.

214—ALLEY RALLY GAME

Objective
This game promotes ball control, sound footwork, and shot placement.

Description
Players are limited to hitting balls back and forth inside the doubles alley. They must find a way to maneuver their feet, strokes, and bodies to keep the ball in play.

Execution
Two players take positions opposite each other in one of the doubles alleys. They use the service line as a boundary line. Players attempt to rally back and forth using only the doubles alley. Players should try to keep 5 balls in play. After accomplishing that, they try to keep 10 to 15 balls in play. After players master that, they play a regular-scoring tennis game inside the alley. When players become comfortable with that method, they can play an entire match.

Variation
Players can hit forehand to forehand, backhand to backhand, or alternate strokes. They play a game, set, or match.

215—WACKY KNEES GAME

Objective
This game promotes speed of foot and having fun.

Description
This game helps players learn how to serve in a wacky way. By placing a ball between the knees, players are prevented from focusing too much on the technical side of serving.

Execution
Players line up across the baseline with 10 balls next to each of them. On cue, each player picks up a ball and places it between the knees. A racket is on the service line in front of each player. On cue, players race to the rackets, pick one up, take the ball out from between the knees, and attempt a serve over the net. If they serve the ball over, they run back to the baseline, pick up another ball, place it between the knees, and so on until they have served all balls over the net. The first player who serves all balls over the net and sits on the baseline wins.

Variation
Players can put the ball under the chin for wacky chin, under the arm for wacky armpits, or between the feet for wacky feet.

216—TORNADO TENNIS GAME

Objective
This game improves hand-eye coordination, balance, footwork, agility, and speed.

Description
Creating a game out of volleying and hitting overheads forces young players to track the incoming ball with more confidence. Young players are usually afraid to volley or hit overheads. They feel as though they are too close to the ball and might be hit by it. When young players think only about playing to beat the other team, their fears of the net seem to float away.

Execution
The instructor splits up the players into two teams and positions them behind the baseline facing the net. The instructor is on the opposite side of the net with a basket of balls. The first two players sprint up to the net, spin around once, split step, hit a forehand volley, spin around in the opposite direction, hit a backhand volley, spin around again in the opposite direction, and hit an overhead. If a player can complete the entire tornado sequence without missing, he or she runs back to the baseline and tags the next player in line. The winning team is the one that first has all its members complete the sequence.

217—HIGHEST SKYSCRAPER GAME

Objective
This game develops hand-eye coordination, speed, and dexterity.

Description
Players learn how to use the quick stepping needed to play tennis. This game also emphasizes team spirit and teamwork.

Execution
Players form two teams positioned behind the baseline. Each team tries to build the highest skyscraper using their rackets and balls between the rackets. The teams start with three rackets with balls between the rackets. Holding the skyscraper together by their grips, they race up to the net and back. If they do not drop any of the balls, they add another ball and racket, race to the net and return, and so on until one team loses control and drops everything.

Variation
Players form two teams and position themselves behind the baseline facing the net. The first two players in line put one ball between their rackets, race forward, and flip the ball over the net. The next pair may go when both relay touches are made. The first team to complete all rounds and take seats at the baseline wins.

218—ICEBREAKER GAME

Objective
This game develops hand-eye coordination and tracking skills.

Description
The game helps players develop good ball and court sense while developing friendly relationships with other tennis players.

Execution
Players are scattered randomly around the court but on the same side. The instructor starts by tossing in the first ball and saying his or her name at the same time. The player who catches it tosses it and says his or her name and so on. Players must remember who the ball was tossed to each time, follow the same sequence, and say that person's name. The instructor starts a second ball and a third ball. The group sees how many balls they can send at one time without making a mistake.

219—SCOOP AND SCOOT GAME

Objective
This game develops racket and ball control.

Description
This game teaches young players what it takes to run down shots.

Execution
Players form two teams and position themselves on the baseline facing the net. A chaser from each team is on the opposite side of the net. A pile of balls and one racket are at the net for each team. The first player runs to the balls, picks one up, and softly hits it to the chaser, who has a bucket or tennis tube. The chaser retrieves the ball and puts it in the bucket. The chaser puts the bucket down and runs to the baseline with the other players, and the next player goes. The player who hit the ball to the chaser puts the racket back by the pile of balls, runs to the other side of the net, and becomes the new chaser. The first team with all the balls in their bucket and seated at the baseline wins.

Variation
Players can use forehands, backhands, or serves.

Tip
Instructors should keep an eye out for crashes with eager players. Markers to designate the start and finish should keep them safe.

220—RACKET RELAY GAME

Objective
This game develops footwork, speed, agility, and conditioning.

Description
Players race against each other to complete tennis tasks in an entertaining way. Getting young players to work on conditioning can be challenging, but when the instructor adds a reward (candy!), they'll love it.

Execution
Players line up in relay formation outside the singles or doubles sideline facing the opposite sideline. Rackets from each team are placed in line along the center service line from the net to the baseline or from baseline to baseline. On cue, the first player from each team races forward, picks up a racket, races around a cone on the opposite sideline, returns, and places the racket back on the center service line. The player races back to the team and tags the next player, who repeats the relay. The winner is the first team to complete the relay and sit behind the sideline.

Variation
The first player brings the racket back to the next player in line, who puts the racket back on the service line while returning from the other sideline, standing the racket on end. Each player carries the same racket. Players sidestep or run backward.

221—HOT POTATO GAME

Objective
This game develops good racket and ball control, hand-eye coordination, and athletic agility.

Description
Players are positioned in a circle so that they can pass the ball from racket to racket. The arrangement allows players to connect with each other and get to know each other in an enjoyable way.

Execution
Players with rackets are arranged around the court in a big circle facing each other. They start bouncing the hot potato (ball) around the circle from player to player without letting the hot potato drop. Players who let the hot potato drop are out. They play until two players are left. Then things really heat up. Hot potato, hot potato, you're out!

Variation
The ball can bounce on the ground or around the circle in any order. Players can face out rather than in.

222—MUNCHKIN SEZ GAME

Objective
This game promotes good racket and ball control. Players learn different tennis strokes, grips, and tennis movement.

Description
This entertaining game mimics the well-known game of Simon Says. Students are required to act out a specific tennis task, which helps them identify with each technique and commit it to memory.

Execution
Players stand around the court, each with a racket and ball. On the cue of "Munchkin sez," each player executes a specific tennis task. Players must hold that position until munchkin sez the next command. Players can't move until the command is given. Those who move must go to the side and perform a tennis exercise. The game continues until one player remains.

Variation
Players execute commands while moving around the court randomly.

223—CRAZY CAPS GAME

Objective
This game develops good racket and ball control and athletic proficiency.

Description
This game works to develop hand-eye coordination and racket and ball control by having players perform tennis ups and downs while chasing other players around the court.

Execution
Players scatter around the court, each holding a racket and a ball. One or more players wear crazy caps. Players move around the court bouncing balls up or down with their rackets. Players with crazy caps attempt to tag the players without caps. Those who don't have the caps try to avoid being tagged. If players wearing the crazy caps lose control over their balls, they lose their crazy caps to the players that tagged them.

Variation
Players can bounce balls in the air or perform other combinations. Players without caps can try to snatch the caps off the heads of the cap wearers.

Tip
Instructors should remind players of good sportsmanship and require them to take the caps off other players' heads gently.

224—CRAZY HITTING GAME

Objective

This game teaches players how to hit different types of spin. It also teaches players how to hit different types of ball spin by incorporating both the visual and auditory receptors.

Description

This game encourages players to move their feet and watch the ball connect with their rackets. Players learn what different types of spin do to the ball and therefore will want to learn the grips and technique needed to hit different types of spin.

Execution

The instructor splits players up into two teams, positioning them behind the baseline or service line. The instructor hits shots with various types of spin to the first player in each line. That player attempts to hit the shot back over the net and onto the court. The team that hits the most balls over the net and in the court wins. Alternatively, the first team to hit 25 shots over the net and onto the court wins.

Variations

Players can practice catching with their hands, a hat, or a bucket. For example, position all players single file behind the center (T) on either the baseline or serviceline. Each player has a hat or bucket to attempt to catch the shot that the instructor hits. This game is an excellent way to teach on-court foot movement coupled with the agility and speed needed in order to catch a tennis ball with topspin on it into a hat or bucket.

Tip

Players should avoid diving to catch the ball with their hands, hats, or buckets. Instructors may want to set boundary lines, such as circles or squares, around each player if the game becomes a little too competitive. Instructors should try to emphasize the positioning of the racket head when connecting with the ball. Players should strike the ball at the precise vertical angle to impart the desired spin on the incoming ball.

225—RED LIGHT! GREEN LIGHT! GAME

Objective

This game teaches players how to manipulate the ball and racket to develop balance and coordination. It helps to develop the "steady head-eyes down" through impact technique. This vital tactic helps players consistently nail the ball with the "sweet spot" of the racket.

Description

This is a great game for a class warm-up or cool-down. The game can also be performed using tennis ups and downs. The instructor should encourage players to watch their own balls and rackets because young players tend to watch everyone else and end up dropping their balls off their rackets. Tell players to "Keep your eagle eyes peeled and focused on the ball."

Execution

The instructor lines up players next to each other on the baseline. Each player places a ball on the strings of his or her racket and tries to balance it on the strings. The instructor yells, "Green light!" While balancing balls on their rackets, the students can run, walk, or skip up toward the net until the instructor yells, "Red light!" Then all activity stops. The first student to reach the net without dropping the ball off his or her racket is the winner.

Variation

Instructors can add another colored light (for example, "Purple light" means that students must spin around while balancing a ball on their rackets). When the instructor yells, "Red light," students should stop, bend down, and touch their toes, while continuing to balance the ball on their racket. If the students drop the ball, they should start over from their original starting position.

Tip

Instructors should be flexible with their lesson plans, varying the activities depending on skills and attentiveness. Players appreciate the enthusiasm of an instructor who demonstrates and participates, so join in on most of your games. Show your players that you can also make mistakes or that you can run, skip, jump, or dance. Show them that if they practice hard enough they too can perform just like you. Be a great example, because your students will learn more, play more, and will never forget who taught them how.

226 — SPUD GAME

Objective

This game reinforces the fundamentals of ground stroking, footwork, directing the ball, and racket and ball control.

Description

Having players combine hitting, thinking, and running adds tremendous fun into learning fundamentals. Players have a chance to hit a ground stroke in play (on the opposite side of the net) or when sprinting a race to win games.

Execution

Players line up across the baseline. Each player gets a number (any number between 1 and 30). All leftover numbers are ghost numbers. The instructor calls out a number. The student with that number runs up to a designated spot and hits a forehand or backhand ground stroke over the net and onto the court. If the student misses the shot, he or she receives the letter *S*. The student receives a letter for each subsequent miss until he or she spells out the word *SPUD*. But that's not the only way students gain letters. Remember the ghost numbers? When the instructor calls out a ghost number, all players must run as fast as they can up to the net, touch it, and then run back to the baseline. The first player to cross the baseline loses a letter, and the last one gains a letter.

Variations

ABC SPUD is played exactly like regular spud. Instead of using numbers, the game uses the 26 letters of the alphabet. When the instructor calls out a letter, the student whose letter has been called runs up to hit either a forehand or backhand and has seven seconds to think of a word that begins with that letter. All other rules stand.

Once players progress to controlling a sustained rally, let the frogs battle it out against the royalty. For example, if a king swats his fly (ball) over the net and a frog swats it back, let the two players continue until one player wins the rally.

Tip

Playing fun tennis games helps players young or old, beginner or veteran, incorporate all of the fundamental stroke techniques for good match play learned and solidified through drilling. Players will get a good sense of competitive play while participating in a stress-free tennis environment.

227—LEAP FROG GAME

Objective

This game develops the fundamentals of ground strokes, footwork, tracking, and hitting an incoming ball.

Description

Having players use their imagination to create a magical kingdom surrounding the tennis court takes the pressure off performance. The players cast themselves in different roles and try to act as their characters while learning the fundamentals of tennis.

Execution

Players line up behind either the baseline or the service line. The instructor informs them that they are now the kings and queens of their castles. Their tennis rackets are fly swatters, and the balls are flies. As long as the kings and the queens swat the flies back over the net, they remain royalty. But if they miss the flies, they turn into frogs! The frogs must run over to the instructor's side of the court, a big lily pad where all the hungry frogs live. The only way for frogs to turn back into royalty is to catch one of the flies hit by a king or queen before the fly rolls off the lily pad into the murky pond surrounding them (anywhere outside the tennis court). The winner is the last remaining king or queen who can successfully swat flies back over the tennis net.

Variation

Once players progress to controlling a sustained rally, let the frogs battle it out against the royalty. For example, if a king swats his fly (ball) over the net and a frog swats it back, let the two players continue until one player wins the rally.

Tip

Instructors and parents should work to develop positive attitudes about competition so that players enjoy the game beyond winning or losing. Helping players learn how to let go of the "need to win" or "desire and fear" attitude will help them concentrate on solely playing and hitting the ball. This causes them to have a sense of tennis integrity or sense of pride in their own game-playing ability as well as their opponents. Playing the *game* of tennis takes priority over the desire to win and the fear of losing.

228—CRUSH A BUG GAME

Objective

This game develops hand-eye coordination, ground-stroking technique, and ball-tracking skills.

Description

Players at the beginning and advanced beginning stages enjoy trying to hit the ball past their opponents. This game introduces mild competition. This is the jump-off point for instructors or parents to teach the beginning player the rules of tennis. Try to incorporate the official tennis scoring, game, and match playing system.

Execution

Players line up behind the center (T) of the service line or baseline. The instructor feeds a forehand or backhand ball for the first player to hit. If the player misses, he or she runs to the other side of the court. In this position the only way the student can get back into the game is by using his or her racket to trap a ball tossed by the instructor or hit over the net by a hitter. A player who accomplishes this switches places with the hitter. The winner is the last player who hits a ball over the net and escapes being trapped by the trappers.

Variation

The Catch a Fly variation is like Crush a Bug except that the instructor mixes up the balls fed, and the students are restricted to a specific part of the court. When the student misses a shot, he or she must run over to the instructor's side of the court. The only way for the player to get back into the game is to catch a ball out of the air hit by a student who is still a hitter. If the player succeeds in catching a ball, he or she takes the place of the hitter. The last player who hits a ball over the net into the correct part of the court without the ball being caught wins.

Tip

The instructor should praise attempts to catch and throw, because very young players are still working on their gross motor skills. Any encouragement by the instructor or parent will help young players progress in their emotional and physical athletic development. Try not to use negatives like "Don't hit that way," or "Stop swinging so fast." Try using positive encouragement like, "That's great, now let's try it this way," or, "Wow, what an arm you have! Now let's see if you can hit the ball into the basket." Always try to turn a negative into a positive and watch how your players young or old respond.

229—BASKETBALL TENNIS GAME

Objective

This game promotes good racket and ball control for hitting balls out in front, hand-eye coordination, and competitive emotional development.

Description

Adding the elements of a basketball game helps players identify with a sport they may be familiar with. This method adds lots of fun, competition, and stimulation for the learning process. This game also helps to develop the "hitting out in front" basic stroke concept. All balls should be hit out in front of the player's torso, in whatever direction the player's torso is facing.

Execution

The instructor divides players into two or more teams. Teams A and B are positioned behind the baseline at the center (T). When the instructor gives the cue, the first player in each line bounces a ball down with the racket to the net and attempts to hit a ground stroke to a specific area marked beforehand by the instructor on the opposite court. The instructor can set points for shots that land in specific parts of the court. Balls that hit the baseline are worth three points, balls that land in no-man's land are worth two points, and so on. The team with the most points wins the game.

Variation

Players hit balls from different areas on the court and use different types of shots. The teaching cart can be the basketball net, and a shot hit directly into the basket can count as a slam jam!

Another variation is to place several buckets around the interior of the singles court or doubles court area, and assign a point value to each bucket. The first player to accumulate 21 points wins the game.

Tip

The instructor should remind players to keep their heads steady and eyes down through impact. This practice promotes consistent contact on or near the center of the strings. This is also a great way to get students to pick up the balls and return them to the teaching cart. Young players get bored with just collecting the balls to put them back in the cart, but if you can make it seem like a game they will never realize they're simply picking up and putting away the balls.

230—CREEPY CRAWLY GAME

Objective

This game develops racket and ball control, dexterity, ball sense, footwork skills, hand-eye coordination, and concentration skills.

Description

Players form a tightly connected line and attempt to pass a tennis ball from one person to the next. When the ball reaches the last person in line, the leader of the line should have sprinted to the end of the line to keep the line progressing forward and the ball passing continuous.

Execution

Players split into two or more teams. Teams are positioned on the baseline, each with a stack of balls beside them. The first player in each line balances a ball on his or her strings and passes it to the next player in line. When the last player gets the ball, the first player in line should sprint back to the end of the line to keep the ball passing moving. Each team creeps and crawls (walks using tiny steps) their way up to the net. When a team reaches the net, a player hits the ball over the net using a service motion, and the team runs back to the baseline to start all over. The first team to hit all their balls over the net and take seats on the baseline wins the game.

Variation

Players use different strokes to hit the ball over the net. Players can also use only their hands and continuously flip the ball up and back over their heads to the player behind them, who catches the ball. Continue the flipping pattern until one player flubs either a catch or flip.

Tip

Have players flip or hit (pop up) soft, low, controllable passes so the player who is receiving the ball can catch and pass with control. Have players bunched together so as to encourage short stepping. Precision footwork is the key to balance and timing when attempting to hit effortlessly, consistently, and with fluidity and tremendous power. A player who bounces quickly on the balls of his or her feet will be mentally prepared for successful play.

231—CATERPILLAR GAME

Objective

This game develops hand-eye coordination, dexterity, teamwork skills, footwork, and good racket and ball control.

Description

The principle of using tiny, tight steps to play tennis is often overlooked. This game helps players feel and experience the type of footwork they need to run, hit, recover, sprint, stop, and quickly change direction during match play.

Execution

The instructor positions one or more teams behind the baseline in relay formation. The first player in the line of each team flips a ball over his or her head to the next team player in line. This player catches the flipped ball on the racket, less the hands, and flips it overhead to the next player in line. The last player in line runs to the front of the line with the ball on the racket. The lines inch forward as players change position. If a team loses control of the ball, they must start from the beginning again. Teams complete a full rotation with players returning to their original positions in line. Teams see how many rotations they can make before dropping the ball.

Variation

Players can pass the ball or racket and ball between the legs, over the shoulder, or alternating over and under. They can try racing up to the net and back using this method. You can make the caterpillar into a millipede, or as long as you can make the "bug." This game is also a great prelesson warm-up if you have six or more players participating.

Tip

This game is also a great icebreaker for new students joining new classes. It encourages awesome communication and teamwork. Helping players to build good teamwork skills through playing group games on the tennis court teaches players much more than just using their individual efforts to succeed or fail. Players learn that combining individual ideas and efforts and coming up with different strategic methods builds lasting friendships and good sportsmanship, all while having fun in the process.

232—LIZARDS HAVE TWO SKINS GAME

Objective

This game develops hand-eye coordination, physical skill, and good racket and ball control. Players will learn good teamwork and communication skills.

Description

This mildly competitive game encourages players to work on strengthening their forearms and hand-eye coordination in an entertaining way. Beginning players discover the fun of hitting the ball with their racket using their own style and strategy. Players will ultimately gain confidence in the use of their feet, hands, eyes, and their ever-changing, developing bodies.

Execution

Team A and team B take the court and flip a coin to decide which team is the stationary team and which team gets to move while bouncing their balls. Players from the team that wins the toss, team A, each have a racket and two balls and are scattered randomly around the court. On the instructor's cue, players from team A move around the court, bouncing the ball in the prescribed manner (ups or downs). Team B waits patiently in place, bouncing their balls, waiting for just one mistake. When a player (from either team) loses control over the first ball, he or she uses the second ball. Players who lose control of their second ball lose their skin (turn). A player can restore his or her skin (turn) if a teammate opts to give the player one of his or her two balls. The team that has the fewest skinless players wins.

Variation

Players can bounce the ball in the air or alternate ups and downs. Have players attempt bouncing the ball on the edge of their racket head or even the butt of the racket.

Tip

To help players focus on watching the ball and not the other players, the instructor should ask them to try to read the number printed on the ball while bouncing it down or up on the racket. How many ball numbers can a player read correctly while practicing tennis ups and downs? Or, how many times can each player bounce the ball down or up or a combination in a row? Instructors can also join in the competition. When players see you performing the task it encourages them to try harder.

233—WONKA-WASH GAME

Objective

This game promotes quick bursts of speed, good footwork, and hand-eye co-ordination.

Description

This game encourages patience when trying to hit under pressure. Players can run, walk fast, or hop up on the their team's pile of balls and attempt a serve into the correct service box. Players who miss keep trying until they get the ball into the service court.

Execution

Players split up into two teams and take positions on the baseline next to each other. On the service line directly in front of each team is a big stack of balls. On the instructor's cue, the first player in line from each team runs up to their pile of balls. The player picks up a ball, spins around the pile, and then hits a serve over the net. If the player succeeds in hitting the ball over the net and into the correct service box, he or she runs to the end of the line while the next player takes off. If the player misses the ball into the net, he or she retrieves the ball, runs back to the service line, and keeps trying until successful. The first team to serve all their balls over the net wins the game.

Variation

Players can hit balls to different areas on the court or use different strokes. There are many different ways to get players who may be having some coordination issues to really feel and connect with the ball. For example, have the players pretend that the ball they will be tossing is a baby bird. Ask that they gently toss the baby bird up to help it fly away. Now ask the player to catch the bird up high with their tennis racket. Or, you can have your players pretend the ball is a planet that they are responsible for placing high into the sky. Then they can land their rocket ship (racket) on that planet. The point is to be creative with your teaching and soon all players will be serving on their own.

Tip

The instructor should encourage students to support a teammate who is having trouble focusing and can't serve or hit the ball over the net. Instructors should remind players that it's perfectly normal to make mistakes during practice – that's what practice is for, to make mistakes and learn how to correct them. If players are attempting to learn a new stroke or shot, throw major support and encouragement their way so the player will be eager to keep trying.

234—FOX AND CHICKEN GAME

Objective

This game promotes quick, evasive reactions on the court and develops agility, speed, and coordination.

Description

This is a wonderful end-of-class game or warm-up game.

Execution

Players divide into two groups and stand in both doubles alleys facing each other. One team is the chickens, and the other team is the foxes. The instructor calls out, "Chicken!" All the foxes must then try to catch the escaping chickens before they make it successfully across the court and into the foxes' den (the opposite doubles alley). Each chicken caught becomes a fox. The last chicken left wins the game.

235—FREEZE-TAG TENNIS GAME

Objective

This game develops racket and ball control, athletic proficiency, and teamwork skills.

Description

This game is played a lot like freeze tag except that tennis players are required to practice a tennis task while attempting to tag other players from the opposing team.

Execution

Players of two opposing teams are scattered randomly around the court, each with a racket and ball in hand. Both teams should designate two or more players as taggers. On cue, all players start moving and bouncing the ball all around the court trying to avoid the other team's taggers. If the ball gets away from a member of team A, that player retrieves it, freezes in place, and bounces the ball while stationary. The frozen player of team A may resume moving if an unfrozen teammate tags him or her. The winner is the last unfrozen player left bouncing the ball around the court.

Variation

Try this game applying the same rules, but using the dexterity ball. Using the dexterity ball helps young players develop quick hands and feet and coordination and increases their tracking skills.

chapter 18

Backboard Drilling Games

The backboard is the tennis player's trusted companion and nemesis at the same time. How many times do players try to beat the backboard? I can't beat the backboard, but I keep trying, and it has made me a far better player. Players will never have a better practice partner than the old reliable backboard. It never misses, and it helps players groove and develop their ground strokes to become better and tougher players. The backboard can be any size or surface as long as balls bounce and return consistently back to the player. Beginners should use an old ball with a slower bounce to give them more control while attempting to rally. Practicing against the backboard improves a player's consistency, placement, depth control, spin, and power. Players of any level can benefit from practicing against the backboard. Here are a few beneficial backboard games that are fun and will help players develop all parts of their game.

236 – KEY TARGETS GAME

Objective
This drill helps develop variety and consistency in serving.

Description
Repetition is key to improving any stroke in tennis. By practicing all types of serves to different targeted areas marked on the backboard, players can work toward perfecting the stroke, gaining control, and building confidence.

Execution
Players should mark three targets on the backboard approximately 7 feet apart and mark a baseline 39 feet from the backboard where they will stand. They practice 75 serves using flat, slice, and topspin serves to the various targets on the deuce and ad side of the wall.

Variation
Players can practice serving into the targets and then playing the return, hitting until they miss.

Tip
When tossing the ball, players should think "gentle push" or "place" instead of "throw" or "toss."

237 – KALEIDOSCOPE GAME

Objective
Players use this drill to develop and improve their volleying skills.

Description
Practicing volleys up against the backboard is daunting at first because players may not be able to control the pace. By starting slowly and hitting softly, players will gain the control and pace they want and need.

Execution
Players position themselves three feet away from the backboard. They start the volley on the forehand side, hitting softly and gradually hitting higher up the wall until the ball is in front of them. Players should remember to use proper footwork when performing this drill, split stepping after each volley. They should try to hit 100 volleys in a row, take a two-minute break, and repeat. They then switch to perform the sequence with the backhand.

Variation
Players can try this sequence using a combination of the forehand and backhand volleys. They can work patterns like two forehand volleys and one backhand volley.

238—YO-YOING GAME

Objective
This drill develops racket dexterity and coordination.

Description
These little ball exercises help players learn how to feel and handle the ball with gentle hands. To hit different types of spin, players must be able to feel the stroke and the ball.

Execution
Players try to do each of the following exercises 50 times in a row. They place a ball on the racket strings, throw the ball against the wall, and use the racket face to catch it. They pass the ball under the right leg and catch the rebound on the racket. They pass the ball under the left leg and catch the rebound on the racket. They pass the ball from behind the back and catch the rebound on the racket.

239—BACKBOARD OVERHEAD GAME

Objective
This drill helps develop early racket preparation and visual judgment for playing the overhead smash.

Description
Players learn to hit with control and confidence by continuously hitting overheads.

Execution
Players hit the ball down into the ground, causing it to rebound off the wall as a lob. They then play an overhead smash for a winner! As they learn to create better lobs off the backboard, they can make the overhead more difficult by requiring themselves to backpedal for the shot. They repeat the exercise, moving forward slightly as they feed the ball to make the overhead even more difficult. They should also practice backhand overhead smashes.

Tip
Players should work on early preparation to prepare for the overhead smash. They should turn their body sideways as soon as they hit the ball into the wall, and keep their weight on the balls of their feet.

240—POISON IVY GAME

Objective
This drill develops control of the direction of shots.

Description
This drill helps players learn how to direct the ball to specific areas on the court and improve ball accuracy while working on consistency during simulated game play.

Execution
Players mark several targets on the backboard with circles or squares. They designate some as poison ivy and others as antidote. Targets should be about the same size as an oversize racket, or one and a half feet square. Keeping the same ball in play, players alternate hitting ground strokes against the backboard until one of them hits a poison ivy circle. When that occurs, the opponent must hit an antidote circle and can hit up to three balls in a row (the same ball is still in play) to accomplish that. If the opponent hits an antidote circle within three balls, no point is scored. If that player misses an antidote with all three balls, he or she accumulates a point. The first player to accumulate five points loses. If a player cannot make a play on the ball, the ball is fed again and play resumes.

Variation
Players can try to use different strokes such as the volley, backhand, or approach shot. Ball control is obviously important with any stroke, so it's good to vary them regularly. Switching up stroke can also be refreshing when players tire of the current stroke.

Tips
Learning to hit specialty shots such as drop volleys requires good feel, coordination, and dexterity of the hand and racket. When practicing any of these games, players should try to incorporate some of the finesse shots into the game. By practicing those shots, players can make them a permanent part of their arsenal of strokes.

Players must know that the direction of any shot in tennis is controlled by the racket face. The ball will go in the direction the strings are facing. When the racket face is looking diagonally across the net the ball will go crosscourt, and when the racket face is looking squarely at the net with the strings parallel to the net the ball will go down the line. Remind players of this simple rule if they are having problems controlling the direction of shots.

241—BACKBOARD SHADOW GAME

Objective

This drill is a fantastic cardiovascular workout that helps develop sound footwork and core strength.

Description

Players get a great cardio workout because the backboard never misses. They also learn how to focus and keep the ball in play.

Execution

Players mark targets to keep teams in their playing areas. The player at the front of the line hits a ball and rotates to the end of the line. The next person in line keeps the same ball in play and rotates. The following players do the same. At the end of one minute the team that has kept the most balls in play wins. Players perform backboard shadowing with volleys or half volleys. Bonus points may be awarded for hitting the target.

242—POP-UP GAME

Objective

This drill helps players learn how to execute and retrieve a lob volley in a point situation.

Description

Lob volleys take good racket control, coordination, timing, and confidence. By hitting with a partner and the backboard, players can acquire tremendous insight into how to hit this shot during simulated play in a controlled and uncontrolled setting.

Execution

Players mark a target area with two lines 10 to 15 feet apart and perpendicular to the backboard. They mark another line 30 to 39 feet from the backboard to create the playing area. The playing area may be adjusted depending on the players' skill level. Two players stand 6 to 10 feet apart and 5 to 7 feet from the backboard. Players hit moderately paced volleys back and forth to each other with each player's ball rebounding off the backboard before reaching the opponent. Once the ball has been in play for three consecutive volleys, each player has the option of hitting a lob volley by hitting a volley higher on the backboard, a shot that will rebound over the opponent's head to an area inside the playing area. The lob retriever has the option of answering the lob with an overhead smash or running the ball down, taking it off the bounce, and playing the shot with a ground stroke. In either case, after retrieving the lob, the player should proceed immediately back to the original position and continue playing the point. A point is over when a ball lands outside the designated area on the court.

243—RACK ATTACK GAME

Objective
This game encourages aggressive play in point situations.

Description
This drill encourages players to think and move the ball around on the court. The player learns how to build points one shot at a time before pouncing on the correct shot to win the point.

Execution
Players create a playing area by marking two lines on the court 20 to 30 feet apart and perpendicular to the backboard. They also mark a line 30 to 40 feet from the backboard and parallel to it. Both players line up behind the horizontal line. Player A bounce hits a ball to the backboard, making the ball land in the playing area on the court. The players then alternate ground strokes until they hit a total of three. At that point players have the option of continuing to hit ground strokes or hitting any other type of shot, including volleys. After the first three shots, any type of shot is allowed as long as the ball rebounds off the backboard and lands in the playing area. A point is over when a player misses a shot. The first player to win 21 points wins the game.

244—SUPERBALL TOUCH GAME

Objective
This game develops a feel for the ball and control of the ball when close to the net (backboard).

Description
This is one of the best ways for players to learn how to control the pace of the ball when attempting to hit touch volleys. Players get a sense of how to relax and use their bodies to hit touch shots.

Execution
Players should draw three to four circle targets on the backboard. Standing at arm's length from the backboard, players volley the ball, keeping the racket no more than one foot from the backboard. They vary the distance within this short range, moving along the wall and keeping control of the ball.

Variation
Players can repeat this exercise using backhand touch volleys.

Tip
When players develop a good sense of feel for the stroke, they should try to add more backspin to the ball. This move changes the trajectory of the shot so that the ball falls more vertically after it crosses the net.

245—MONKEY SEE, MONKEY DO GAME

Objective

This drill helps develop and groove a variety of shots.

Description

This exercise helps players groove their ground strokes, practice quick foot-work, quicken their reflexes, and play out points.

Execution

Players mark two vertical lines 10 to 15 feet apart on the backboard. Two play-ers position themselves 15 to 25 feet from the backboard, each in front of one of the vertical lines. Player A bounce feeds the ball so that it lands between the lines on the backboard and rebounds to any spot on the court. Player B responds by playing the same ball with any type of shot (ground stroke, half volley, volley, approach shot) and any type of spin. Player A must keep the ball in play by executing the same type of shot with the same type of spin. Player B then keeps the ball in play by hitting another shot, which player A must duplicate. The point ends if player B hits a shot outside the designated line area or if player A fails to duplicate player B's shot. After every point, the players change roles. The first player to earn 15 points wins.

Glossary

This is the official USTA tennis glossary. Although some of the terms may not appear in this book, players should become familiar with them if they plan to play and compete in the game of tennis. Players may hear these terms during tennis lessons and tennis tournaments.

ace—A ball served so well that the opponent has no chance to touch or return it.

ad—Short for "advantage," it is the first point scored after deuce. If the serving side scores, it is "ad in"; if the receiving side scores, it is "ad out."

ad court—The left-handed service court so called because an ad score is served there.

all—An even score—30-all, 3-all, and so on.

alley—The area on either side of the singles court that enlarges the width of the court for doubles. Each alley is 4 1/2 feet wide.

American twist—A spin serve that causes the ball to bounce high and in the opposite direction from which it was originally traveling.

angle shot—A ball hit to an extreme angle across the court.

approach—A shot behind which a player comes to the net.

attack drive—An aggressive approach shot.

australian doubles—Doubles in which the point begins with the server and server's partner on the same right or left side of the court

backcourt—The area between the service line and the baseline.

backhand—The stroke used to return balls hit to the left of a right-handed player or to the right of a left-handed player.

backspin—The ball spins from bottom to top (counterclockwise), applied by hitting down and through the ball. Also called "underpin." See also slice and chop.

backswing—The initial part of any swing. The act of bringing the racket back to prepare for the forward swing.

ball person—During competition, a person who retrieves balls for the players.

Adapted, by permission, from USPTA, 2001, *The Complete Guide to United States Professional Tennis Association Membership – Section V/Resources for the Tennis Teacher* (USPTA World Headquarters: Houston, TX) 214-218.

baseline—The end boundary line of a tennis court, located 39 feet from the net.

bevel—The tilt or slant of the racket face.

boron—An expensive, extremely durable material used to manufacture racket frames.

break service—To win a game in which the opponent serves.

bye—In competition, the situation in which a player is not required to play in a particular round.

cannonball—A hard, flat serve.

center mark—The short line that bisects the center of the baseline.

center service line—The line that is perpendicular to the net and divides the two service courts.

center strap—A strap in the center of the net, anchored to the ground to hold the net secure at the height of three feet.

check "pause"—The moment when both feet land together and "split" apart when approaching the net as the opponent is returning the ball.

chip—A modified slice used primarily in doubles to return a serve. A chip requires a short swing, which allows the receiver to move in close to return.

choke up—To grip the racket up higher on the handle.

chop—A backspin shot in which the racket moves down through the ball at an angle greater than 45 degrees.

closed face—The angle of the hitting face of the racket when it is turned down toward the court.

code, the—A supplement to the rules of tennis that specifically defines etiquette parameters such as "gamesmanship" and line call responsibilities.

composite—A racket frame reinforced with graphite, fiberglass, or boron.

consolation—A tournament in which first-round losers continue to play in a losers' tournament.

crosscourt shot—A shot in which the ball travels diagonally across the net, from one sideline of the court to the other.

deep shot—A shot that bounces near the baseline (near the service line on a serve).

default—Failure to complete a scheduled match in a tournament; a defaulting player forfeits her or his position.

deuce—A score of 40-40 (the score is tied and each side has at least three points).

deuce court—The right-hand court is called the deuce court. The ball is served there on a deuce score.

dink—A ball returned so that it floats across the net with extreme softness.

double elimination—A tournament in which a player or team must lose twice before being eliminated.

double fault—The failure of both service attempts to be good. It costs a point.

doubles—A game or match with four players, two on each team.

draw—The means of establishing who plays whom in a tournament.

drive—An offensive ball hit with force.

drop shot—A softly hit shot that barely travels over the net.

drop volley—A drop shot that is volleyed before it bounces.

earned point—A point won through skillful playing rather than through an opponent's mistake.

eastern grip—The forehand and backhand grips presented in this text as the standard basic forehand and backhand grips.

elimination—A tournament in which a player is eliminated when defeated.

error—A point achieved through an obvious mistake rather than through skillful playing.

face—The hitting surface of the racket.

fast court—A court with a smooth surface, which causes the ball to bounce quick and low.

fault—An improper hit generally thought of as a service error.

fifteen—The first point won by a player or team.

flat shot—A shot that travels in a straight line with little arc and little spin.

floater—A ball that moves slowly across the net in a high trajectory.

foot fault—A fault resulting from the server stepping on the baseline, or into the playing court, before hitting the ball during the serve, or from a player standing beyond the sideline or touching the wrong side of the center mark before the ball is served.

forcing shot—A ball hit with exceptional power. A play in which, because of the speed and placement of the shot, the opponent is pulled out of position.

forecourt—The area between the net and the service line.

forehand—The stroke used to return balls hit to the right of a right-handed player or to the left of a left-handed player.

forehand court—For a right-handed player, the right-hand side of the court. For a left-handed player, the left-hand side of the court.

forty—The score when a player or team has won three points.

frame—The part of the racket that holds the strings.

game—That part of a set that is completed when one player or side wins four points, or wins two consecutive points after deuce.

graphite—Expensive fibers used to produce extra-strength racket frames.

grip—The method of holding the racket handle; the term given the covering on the handle.

ground stroke—Forehand or backhand stroke made after the ball has bounced.

gut—Racket strings made from animal intestines.

half volley—Hitting the ball immediately after it bounces.

handle—The part of the racket that is gripped in the hand.

head—The part of the racket used to hit the ball, including the frame and strings.

hold serve—To win a game in which one was server.

kill—To smash the ball down hard.

let—A point replayed because of interference; a serve that hits the top of the net but is otherwise good.

linesperson—In competition, a person responsible for calling balls that land outside the court.

lob—A ball hit high enough in the air to clear the net, usually by at least 10 feet, and intended to pass over the head of the net player.

love—Zero or no score.

love game—A game in which the winner never lost a point.

love set—A set in which the winner has won all games.

match—Singles or doubles play consisting of two out of three sets for all women's and most men's matches, or three out of five sets for many men's championship matches and tournaments.

match point—The game point that, if won, also will win the match for a player or team.

midcourt—The general area in the center of the playing court, midway between the net and baseline. Many balls bounce at the player's feet in this area; therefore, the player can be unusually vulnerable.

midsize—A racket head of approximately 85 to 100 square inches. Smaller than an oversize racket.

mix up—To vary the types of shots attempted.

national tennis rating system—A description of different tennis skills that helps the player to "self place" himself or herself at the correct ability level.

net game—The play at net. Also called "net play."

net person—A player positioned at the net.

no ad—Scoring system in which the winner is the first player or team to score four points.

nylon—A type of synthetic racket string.

open face—The angle of the hitting face of the racket when it is turned up, away from the court surface.

opening—A court position that allows an opponent a good chance to win the point.

orthotics—An artificial material that is inserted freely into footwear to add support to the arches of the feet and align the body more efficiently.

out—A ball landing outside the playing court.

overhead smash—See smash.

oversize—Refers to the largest of racket heads, which are 100 square inches or more. Larger than a midsize.

overspin—See topspin.

pace—The speed or spin of a ball, which makes it bounce quickly.

passing shot—A ball hit out of reach of a net player.

percentage tennis—Conservative tennis that emphasizes cutting down on unnecessary errors and on errors at critical points.

place—To hit the ball to a desired area.

placement—A shot placed so accurately that an opponent cannot be expected to return it effectively.

poach—A doubles strategy in which the net player moves over to the partner's side of the court to make a volley.

point penalty system—A penalty system designed to enforce fair play and good sportsmanship.

rally—Play in exclusion of the serve.

retrieve—A good return of a difficult shot.

round robin—A tournament in which every player plays every other player.

seed—To arrange tournament matches so that top players don't play each other until the final rounds.

semiwestern grip—A forehand grip used by many players. The hand is turned on the racket handle from the eastern forehand grip toward the right. This grip encourages extra topspin on the forehand.

serve (service)—Method of starting a point.

service line—The line that marks the base of the service court, parallel to the baseline and 21 feet from the net.

set—The part of a match that is completed when one player or side wins at least six games and is ahead by at least two games, or has won the tiebreaker.

set point—The game point that, if won, also will win the set for a player or team.

sidespin—A shot in which the ball spins to the side and bounces to the side. The sidespin slice is one of the most common types of serve.

singles—A match between two players.

slice—A backspin shot hit with the racket traveling down through the ball at less than a 45-degree angle with the court. See also chip.

slow court—A court with a rough surface, which tends to make the ball bounce rather high and slow.

smash—A hard-hit overhead shot.

spin—Rotation of the ball caused by hitting it at an angle. See topspin, sidespin, and backspin.

straight sets—A match in which the winner has won all sets.

string tension—Describes the tautness of the racket strings. Measured in pounds of weight.

sudden death—In no-ad scoring, when the score reaches 3-all.

synthetic gut—A racket "string" composed of several fibers of a synthetic material (not actually gut) twisted together.

tape—The fabric band that stretches across the top of the net; the lines of a clay court. Lead tape is weighted tape that is applied to the head of a racket to make it heavier.

tennis elbow—A painful condition of the elbow joint commonly caused by hyperextension of the elbow or by excessive wrist action in tennis play.

thirty—The score when a player or team has won two points.

throat—The part of the racket between the handle and the head.

tiebreaker—When the score in any set reaches 6 games all, a 12-point scoring system is used to determine the winner of the set. (A 9-point tiebreaker is also often used.)

topspin—Spin of the ball from top to bottom, caused by hitting up and through the ball. It makes the ball bounce fast and long and is used on most ground strokes.

trajectory—The flight of the ball in relation to the top of the net.

umpire—The person who officiates matches.

undercut—A backspin caused by hitting down through the ball.

underspin—See backspin, slice, and chop.

unseeded—The players not favored to win nor given any special place on draw in a tournament.

VASSS—A no-ad, sudden death scoring system used extensively in the 1970s and 1980s. (No longer used in international competition.)

volley—To hit the ball before it bounces.

wide-body—A racket frame with a head substantially larger (thicker) than its throat.

About the Author

Tina Hoskins is a former professional player on the Women's Tennis Association (WTA) and satellite tours and is a certified professional from the United States Professional Tennis Association (USPTA). She has trained and traveled with some top pros, including Lori McNiel, Zina Garrison, and Rodney Harmon.

Hoskins has more than 30 years of experience in both playing and teaching tennis to all age groups and ability levels. She has helped many young players achieve USTA rankings, with two of her top students achieving national rankings. For the past 10 years, Hoskins has worked as the head tennis instructor at a prestigious racket club in New Jersey. She is also the owner and director of her own business, Future Stars Tennis.